THE SUBMERGED STATE

CHICAGO STUDIES IN AMERICAN POLITICS

A series edited by Benjamin I. Page, Susan Herbst, Lawrence R. Jacobs, and James Druckman

THE SUBMERGED STATE

HOW INVISIBLE GOVERNMENT POLICIES
UNDERMINE AMERICAN DEMOCRACY

SUZANNE METTLER

The University of Chicago Press   Chicago and London

SUZANNE METTLER is the Clinton Rossiter Professor of American Institutions at Cornell University. Her most recent book is *Soldiers to Citizens: The G.I. Bill and the Making of the Greatest Generation.*

The University of Chicago Press, Chicago 60637
The University of Chicago Press, Ltd., London
© 2011 by The University of Chicago
All rights reserved. Published 2011.
Printed in the United States of America

20 19 18 17 16 15   4 5 6 7 8 9 10

ISBN-13: 978-0-226-52164-0 (cloth)
ISBN-10: 0-226-52164-8 (cloth)
ISBN-13: 978-0-226-52165-7 (paper)
ISBN-10: 0-226-52165-6 (paper)

Library of Congress Cataloging-in-Publication Data

Mettler, Suzanne.
  The submerged state: how invisible government policies undermine American democracy / Suzanne Mettler.
      p. cm. — (Chicago studies in American politics)
  Includes bibliographical references and index.
  ISBN-13: 978-0-226-52164-0 (cloth: alk. paper)
  ISBN-10: 0-226-52164-8 (cloth: alk. paper)
  ISBN-13: 978-0-226-52165-7 (pbk.: alk. paper)
      ISBN-10: 0-226-52165-6 (pbk.: alk. paper) 1. United States—Social policy—Public opinion. 2. Public welfare—United States—Public opinion. 3. United States—Politics and government—Public opinion. 4. Americans—Attitudes. 5. United States—Social policy. 6. Public welfare—United States. 7. United States—Politics and government—21st century. 8. Democracy—United States. I. Title.
  HN59.2.M485 2011
  320.60973—dc23   2011017776

♾ This paper meets the requirements of ANSI/NISO Z39.48-1992 (Permanence of Paper).

For Sophie

CONTENTS

INTRODUCTION

Confronting the Submerged State

The teeming crowds of supporters who had cheered candidate Barack Obama's agenda for "change you can believe in" receded quickly. The 2008 presidential election had energized Americans who had never participated in politics before, particularly among the young and minorities, and it had attracted the interest and hopes of many independents, people who are usually less engaged in the political process. Once elected, the young president held to his word and pursued transformations in American social policy—health care reform, new tax breaks, and enhanced aid to college students—that vast majorities of Americans had long told pollsters they favored.[1] Despite the usual travails of the legislative process, exacerbated in 2009 and 2010 by greater political polarization in Congress than at any other point in the post–World War II period, within fifteen months Obama had already achieved much of what he set out to do on these issues.[2] Yet Americans generally seemed unimpressed and increasingly disillusioned. The problem was that most of what had been accomplished could not be seen: it remained invisible to average citizens.

The public had no trouble noticing the jockeying of special interests that sought favored treatment in legislation—that was plain to see—but majorities of Americans remained unaware of the contents of the president's signature achievements, and they lacked basic understanding of how they and their families might be affected by them. The first major piece of legislation that Obama had signed into law, the stimulus bill of February 2009, included a vast array of tax cuts: they totaled $288 billion, 37 percent of the cost of the entire bill.[3] Among them, the Making Work Pay Tax Credit, one of his campaign promises, reduced income taxes for 95 percent of all working Americans. Yet one year after the law went into effect, when pollsters queried the public about whether the Obama administration had raised or lowered taxes for most Americans, only 12 percent answered correctly that taxes had decreased; 53 percent mistakenly thought taxes had stayed the same; and 24 percent even believed they had increased![4] Health care reform represented Obama's chief policy goal, and he expended a vast amount of political capital in pursuing it over his first fifteen months in office. But in April 2010, just weeks after he signed the health care bill that extended coverage to the vast majority of working-age Americans and prohibited insurance companies from denying coverage to people who were ill, 55 percent of the public reported that they would describe their feelings about it as "confused."[5] That same legislative package also contained sweeping changes in student aid policy that aimed to help more people attend college and complete degrees. Yet when Americans were asked how much they had heard about these changes, only 26 percent reported "a lot," while 40 percent said "a little," and fully 34 percent said "nothing at all."[6] All told, the public seemed largely oblivious to the president's major policy accomplishments.

While many who had voted for Obama grew complacent, grassroots mobilization emerged from another quarter, the insurgent Tea Party movement. Wielding placards at protests on tax day, town hall meetings, and other public events, its supporters decried what they termed "government takeovers" of health care and student loans. At a gathering in Simpsonville, South Carolina, in August 2009, one man told Republican Representative Robert Inglis, "Keep your government hands off my Medicare." Inglis said later, "I had to politely explain that 'Actually, sir, your health care is being provided by the government,' but he wasn't having any of it."[7] While as of March 2010 only 13 percent of Americans reported that they considered themselves "part of the Tea Party movement," nonetheless the frustration that it embodied resonated with growing numbers of Americans: 28 percent considered themselves supporters.[8]

With the content of Obama's legislative accomplishments appearing so opaque and incomprehensible even as the calls of opponents resonated loud and clear, most Americans registered reactions that were tepid at best, and many grew increasingly hostile. By the fall of 2010, 61 percent of likely voters told pollsters they favored repeal of health care reform.[9] It was a sharp contrast to the warm reception given to sweeping social welfare laws achieved by earlier presidents. After Franklin D. Roosevelt signed into law the Social Security Act of 1935, 68 percent of the public voiced support for its "contributory old age insurance plan . . . which requires employers and workers to make equal contributions to workers' pensions"—even though its benefits were not scheduled to begin for six years.[10] When Congress passed Lyndon Baines Johnson's plan for Medicare in 1965, strong majorities repeatedly said they approved of it, as high as 82 percent in a December survey that year.[11] Until Obama's presidency, perhaps never before had major laws that aimed to improve the lives of vast numbers of ordinary Americans gone so unrecognized and unappreciated by so many.

What explains the public's reticence, frustration, and confusion? Certainly its reactions owe partly to the worst economic conditions since the Great Depression, with more than two years of near 10 percent unemployment. Some of the lackluster response was inevitable, furthermore, given the sheer scope and complexity of the policy tasks Obama took on. And a share of the blame belongs to his administration's own public relations efforts, which many observers considered underwhelming. Yet while each of these commonly cited factors undeniably played a role, they do not, by themselves, explain Americans' blasé response to major social policy accomplishments that reflected broadly shared values. Historical comparisons make this evident. The public voiced its high approval for the Social Security Act of 1935, for example, when the nation was still mired in the Great Depression and when twice the proportion of Americans, 20 percent, remained jobless. That legislation was also multifaceted and complex, and it was even more novel for the United States than the 2010 health care package, marking the first major involvement of the U.S. federal government in social provision for people besides veterans and their relatives.

The main difference confronted by Obama emanated from the type of policies that he sought to reform, ones that generate particularly formidable obstacles. Any leader who seeks to transform "politics as usual" is bound to confront resistance—challenges emanating from the policies, practices, and institutions already in place.[12] But the nature and difficulty of the task vary depending on the particular goals that reformers select and the historical context in which they pursue them. Roosevelt confronted a political landscape that presented its own challenges—not least, a Supreme Court that served as a major roadblock to his policy ambitions. His administration had to attempt to fashion policies that would circumvent the Court's reach and to build as much as possible on what already existed, such as social policies adopted by some states. But Obama's policy agenda, in the current political context, requires him to engage in a struggle more akin to that undertaken by Progressive Era reformers, who had to destroy or reconstitute deeply entrenched relationships if they were to achieve change.[13] He could not follow the path of Roosevelt, finding a way *around* political obstacles or merely building on top of what existed; rather, he had to find ways to work *through* them, by either obliterating them or restructuring them.

This is because Obama, given his policy agenda, had steered directly into the looming precipice of the *submerged state*: existing policies that lay beneath the surface of U.S. market institutions and within the federal tax system. Contrary to opponents' charges that his agenda involved the encroachment of the federal government into private matters, Obama was actually attempting to restructure a dense thicket of long-established public policies, but ones that are largely invisible to most Americans—and that are extremely resistant to change. Efforts to transform these policies, which have become entrenched fixtures of modern governance, generate a deeply conflictual politics that routinely alienates the public, hindering chances of success or sustainability of the reforms.

The "submerged state" includes a conglomeration of federal policies that function by providing incentives, subsidies, or payments to private organizations or households to encourage or reimburse them for conducting activities deemed to serve a public purpose. Over the past thirty years, American political discourse has been dominated by a conservative public philosophy, one that espouses the virtues of small government. Its values have been pursued in part through efforts to scale back traditional forms of social provision, meaning visible benefits administered fairly directly by government. In the case of some programs geared to the young or working-age people, the value of average benefits has withered and coverage has grown more restrictive.[14] Ironically, however, the more dramatic change over this period has been the flourishing of the policies of the submerged state, which operate through indirect means such as tax breaks to households or payments to private actors who provide services. Since 1980 these policies have proliferated in number, and the average size of their benefits has expanded dramatically.

Most of these ascendant policies function in a way that directly contradicts Americans' expectations of social welfare policies: they shower their largest benefits on the most affluent Americans. Take the Home Mortgage Interest Deduction (HMID), for example, which is currently the nation's most expensive social tax break aside from the tax-free status of employer-provided health coverage. Let us assume that a family buys a median-value home and to finance it borrows $230,000 at an interest rate of 6.25 percent for thirty years. The richer the household, the larger the benefit: in the first year, the average family, with an income between $16,751 and $68,000, would owe around $3,619 less in taxes; those in the next income group, with earnings up to $137,300, would reap an extra $5,146; and so forth, on up to the wealthiest 2 percent of families, with incomes over $373,650, who would enjoy a savings of $6,673. Of course, in reality, these differences are likely to be much greater. Low- to moderate-income Americans usually do not have enough deductions to itemize, so they would forgo this benefit and receive instead only the standard deduction. Meanwhile, the most affluent are likely to purchase far more expensive homes; if a family in the top income category opts for a more upscale home and borrows $500,000 for a mortgage, it will reap a benefit of $14,506 from the HMID; if this family purchases a truly exclusive property and borrows $1 million for a mortgage, it will qualify to keep a whopping $29,012![15] This pattern of upward redistribution is repeated in numerous other policies of the submerged state: federal largesse is allocated disproportionately to the nation's most well-off households. Such policies consume a sizable portion of revenues and leave scarce resources available for programs that genuinely aid low- and middle-income Americans.

Yet despite their growing size, scope, and tendency to channel government benefits toward the wealthy, the policies of the submerged state remain largely invisible to ordinary Americans: indeed, their hallmark is the way they obscure government's role from the view of the general public, including those who number among their beneficiaries. Even when people stare directly at these policies, many perceive only a freely functioning market system at work. They understand neither what is at stake in reform efforts nor the significance of their success. As a result, the charge leveled by opponents of reforms—that they amount to "government takeovers"—though blatantly inaccurate, makes many Americans at least uncomfortable with policy changes, if not openly hostile toward them.

Exacerbating these challenges, at the same time as the submerged state renders the electorate oblivious and passive, it actually promotes vested interests, and it has done so especially over the past two decades. The finance, real estate, and insurance industries all thrived until the recent recession, and in turn they invested heavily in strengthening their political capacity, making them better poised to protect the policies that have favored them. As a result, reform has required public officials to engage in outright combat or deal making with powerful organizations. Such politics disgust most Americans and hardly epitomize the kind of change Obama's supporters expected when he won office.

Other presidents over the past century focused their energies on legislative battles that were far more visible and thus more comprehensible to the public. Towering figures such as Roosevelt and Johnson seized the power of the "bully pulpit" to create the major direct social programs of the New Deal and the Great Society. More recently, presidents have sought to engage in retrenchment, efforts to terminate or to reduce dramatically the size of programs, but here again they concentrated on visible forms of governance. Ronald Reagan took the lead on this approach, telling the nation, "Government is not the solution to our problem; government is the problem."[16] While he failed to abolish full programs, some were curtailed in scope, and benefits stagnated in several that were not protected by mandatory automatic increases. Early in his presidency, Bill Clinton did set out to restructure some components of the submerged state but met with little success, failing at health care reform and achieving only a modest beginning on student loan reform. Thereafter, he turned instead to the highly visible task of attempting to "end welfare as we know it," while simultaneously enlarging the submerged state through new and expanded tax breaks. By contrast to all of these, Obama took on an especially daunting agenda: he prioritized an entire set of social policy issues that each required transformation of the submerged state in order to be accomplished.

Against great odds, Obama has largely succeeded in these pursuits, achieving both health care reform and major student aid legislation. Yet even these and other new policies he has signed into law still cloak government activity in ways that may make it largely imperceptible to most citizens. Their designs hinder Obama's ability to accomplish the broader goals he articulated during his campaign, namely, "reclaiming the meaning of citizenship, restoring our common sense of purpose," and to "restore the vital trust between people and their government."[17] The problem is not simply the typical policy complexity that alienates the public; rather, policies of the submerged state obscure the role of the government and exaggerate that of the market, leaving citizens unaware of how power operates, unable to form meaningful opinions, and incapable, therefore, of voicing their views accordingly.

American politics today is ensnared in the paradox of the submerged state. Our government is integrally intertwined with everyday life from health care to housing, but in forms that often elude our vision: governance appears "stateless" because it operates indirectly, through subsidizing private actors. Thus, many Americans express disdain for government social spending, incognizant that they themselves benefit from it. Even if they do realize that benefits they utilize emanate from government, often they fail to recognize them as "social programs." People are therefore easily seduced by calls for smaller government—while taking for granted public programs on which they themselves rely.[18] Meanwhile, economic inequality has soared in the United States over the past forty years, reaching levels not seen since 1929, yet over this same period, policymakers have adamantly protected submerged state policies that bestow their greatest rewards on the affluent.[19] Ordinary citizens fail to realize the upward bias of such policies. Political leaders who do seek to reform them, to make their benefits more accessible to Americans of low and moderate incomes, face charges of mounting a "government takeover." If against the odds they manage to succeed, the policies achieved, especially if they still cloak government's role, prove difficult to sustain.

Change is possible, however. As this book will show, we can expose the submerged state, reveal governance, and consequently enable citizens to become more engaged and active, reclaiming their voice in the political process. In order to make it possible to carry out reform, first policymakers must reconfigure the role of vested interests. To make reform meaningful, they must alter policies in order to ameliorate their bias toward the affluent. These changes alone, however, will be hard to achieve and even more difficult to sustain, and they will thwart the renewal of citizenship, unless leaders can transform policies to reveal to ordinary Americans their existence and basic effects. To facilitate this, specific strategies must be adopted at the stages of both policy enactment and subsequent implementation. Through policy design and delivery, as well as political communication, policymakers can shift the balance between visible and hidden policies, foster basic awareness of government, and broaden participation in politics.

As long as the submerged state persists in its shrouded form, American democracy is imperiled. Contrary to popular claims, the threat to self-governance is not the size of government, but rather the hidden form so much of its growth has assumed, and the ways in which it channels public resources predominantly to wealthy Americans and privileged industries. We can reclaim governance, however, making it more visible and comprehensible to ordinary Americans, and using policies to ameliorate rather than to exacerbate inequality. With political will and purposeful action, public policy can be refashioned to revitalize democracy.

1 · GOVERNANCE UNSEEN

When Senator Mary Landrieu held a town hall meeting in Louisiana in the summer of 2009 in order to hear her constituents' views on health care reform, she encountered a boisterous crowd. One man stood up, waving a copy of the U.S. Constitution, and asked, "Where does the federal government get any right to stick its hands anywhere in the health care system?"[1] Members of Congress heard similar sentiments expressed at such meetings across the nation. Meanwhile, letters to the editor in newspapers throughout the country contained protestations like that voiced by Ohio resident Ray Brown, who wrote to the *Columbia Dispatch*: "There are no circumstances on this Earth under which we should let our government have anything at all to do with our excellent health-care system."[2] In each case, opponents of reform implied that the U.S. health care system as we know it was borne and persists *sui generis*, a natural development that has been nurtured only by the market economy.

Such characterizations are, quite simply, wrong. As Senator Landrieu explained patiently to the man who questioned her, "Some aspects of our system are nationalized," noting that government programs such as Medicare and Medicaid cover a significant portion of the population, nearly one in three people.[3] She could have explained, further, that the so-called "private" insurance plans provided by employers, through which 59 percent of Americans under age sixty-five receive insurance, are subsidized by government, which privileges them with tax-exempt status.[4] She might have added that the construction of vast numbers of the nation's hospitals was funded by a federal policy enacted in 1948, signed into law by President Harry Truman.[5] Or that a significant portion of students in the nation's medical and nursing schools are funded by federal scholarships.[6]

In fact, the health care system experienced by Americans of the early twenty-first century has been fostered by public policy and highly subsidized by government spending for three-quarters of a century. It is fairly well known that the United States spends more per capita on health care than any other nation; in 2009 this amounted to $2.5 trillion, or 17.6 percent of GDP.[7] Less commonly known is the fact that government itself foots most of the bill—some estimate 56 percent, amounting to more than in any other country.[8] Remarkably, however, many Americans have been largely unaware of government's substantial role in health care, and therefore reform legislation in 2009–10 appeared to them to be a startling new and foreign intervention into a system that belonged mostly if not entirely to the private sector.

The misunderstanding that many people possess about health care policy is unsurprising, however, because much of it—like other areas of contemporary social provision—is embedded within the submerged state. When most people think of government programs, they likely envision cavernous, austere buildings located in the vicinity of Washington, D.C., filled with bureaucrats sitting in cubicles who directly oversee the delivery of goods and services to citizens, as exemplified by Social Security. Many would also acknowledge that states and local governments often play the role of "supporting actors," carrying out much of the day-to-day work of the federal government by following its mandates and dispensing its funds, for example, in unemployment insurance or welfare offices. But, in fact, much of the activity financed by the federal government today fits neither of those standard descriptions. Rather, it disguises or subverts government's role, making the real actors appear to be those in the market or private sector—whether individuals, households, organizations, or businesses. The mechanisms or tools through which such activities occur have proliferated to include a great variety, such as loans subsidized and guaranteed by government but offered through private banks and government-sponsored enterprises; social benefits in the form of tax incentives and tax breaks for those engaging in activities that government wishes to reward; and benefits and services provided by nonprofits and private third-party organizations that are subsidized or "contracted out" by government.[9]

Take student loans, for example. Several years ago, while teaching an undergraduate course on public policy, I included student loans among a list of government social programs. One student objected, saying, "But student loans shouldn't be called a social program! I'm paying for my tuition with student loans and I got them through a bank—not a government agency. And I have to pay them back after I graduate, with interest." Another student quickly countered the first, saying, "But if any of us just went to a bank ourselves and applied for a regular loan—not a student loan guaranteed by government—they probably wouldn't be willing to lend to us. At our age, we don't look like very safe bets for paying back what we borrow. And even if they did lend to us, the loan would cost us a good deal more than it does with government's help." A lively discussion ensued, reflecting different understandings of how student loans operate and different views of the characteristics that define public policies.

These disparities in perceptions owe to the fact that student loans, like much of U.S. health care policy, have long operated primarily by subsidizing private actors to provide social benefits. In the 1960s, policymakers sought means to make college affordable for more students. Banks were typically reluctant to loan to students, considering them a bad risk, and when they did, they imposed high interest rates, typically ranging from 11 to 14 percent and above.[10] The Higher Education Act of 1965, signed into law by Johnson, established the Guaranteed Student Loan Program, giving banks incentives to lend to students at lower rates of interest. It did so by offering that the federal government would pay half the interest on such loans and would guarantee them, promising to repay them entirely if a borrower defaulted. In 1972 policymakers provided further impetus to student lending by creating the Student Loan Marketing Association (SLM, otherwise known as "Sallie Mae"), a "government-sponsored enterprise," meaning that while being privately owned and operated, it would enjoy special privileges—flowing from tax benefits and special regulatory treatment—unavailable to any competitor.[11] In the decades since, student lending became a lucrative business, attracting many banks to participate.

The amounts borrowed annually through these government-subsidized and government-guaranteed loans, renamed as Family Federal Education Loans (FFEL), escalated rapidly, as shown in figure 1.1. Even after Clinton's reform effort in 1993 led to the beginnings of "direct lending," in which government itself made loans using federal capital rather than subsidizing lenders to do so, the well-established bank-based system still continued to predominate, making 80 percent of all loans until the credit crisis hit in 2008.[12] The banks and Sallie Mae possessed marketing power lacked by the U.S. Department of Education, granting them greater leverage in promoting their products to students. In addition, their ability to offer perks and benefits to financial aid offices on college campuses in many cases helped them to secure the privileged status of "preferred lenders," a practice eventually curtailed after an investigation by New York Attorney General Andrew Cuomo.[13]

Not surprisingly, then, even many student loan beneficiaries themselves perceived the program to be private rather than public. A 2008

FIGURE 1.1. U.S Federal Student Loans: Bank-Based, Government Subsidized versus Direct, 1985–2009 (2009 Dollars)

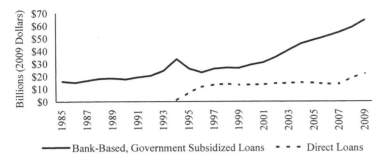

―――Bank-Based, Government Subsidized Loans   ▪ ▪ ▪ Direct Loans

Source: National Center for Education Statistics, U.S. Department of Education, "Federal Support and Estimated Federal Tax Expenditures for Education, by Category: Selected Fiscal Years, 1965 through 2009," *Digest of Education Statistics* (2009), http://nces.ed.gov/programs/digest/d09/tables/dt09_373.asp.

survey asked such individuals, "Do you think of student loans primarily as a public program—that is, belonging to government—or as a private program, that is, belonging to lenders, banks, or academic institutions?" Half of respondents—50 percent—reported that they viewed the program as private, only 43 percent described it as public, and the remainder volunteered that it was both, equally. Despite the fact that such loans would not be available without government—which took the initiative to encourage lending, provided generous subsidies to lenders, and bore the risk of defaults—most users did not perceive its role.[14] These citizens, like my undergraduate recipients of such loans, had the quintessential experience of the submerged state: it benefited them, providing opportunities and relieving financial burdens, *without them even knowing it.*

Several of our most expensive federal social policies today are situated within the income tax system. "Social tax expenditures," as they have been termed formally in federal budgeting parlance since 1969, or "tax breaks" or "tax loopholes," as they are more commonly known, permit particular households to pay less in taxes because they are either involved in some kind of activity or they belong to a class of persons that policymakers deem worthy of public support.[15] Rather than government sending checks to people, as is the case for Social Security or Temporary Assistance for Needy Families, instead families or individuals receive social benefits either in the form of smaller tax bills or refunds from the Internal Revenue Service. Today, as seen in figure 1.2, the largest social tax expenditure emanates from the nontaxable nature of health insurance benefit provided

FIGURE 1.2. Largest Social Tax Expenditures: Year Enacted and Estimated Cost in 2011 (Billions of Dollars)

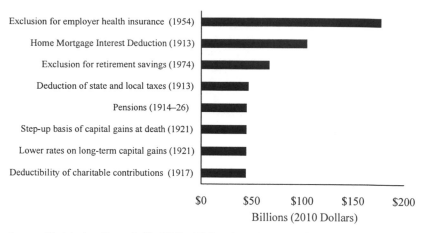

Exclusion for employer health insurance (1954)

Home Mortgage Interest Deduction (1913)

Exclusion for retirement savings (1974)

Deduction of state and local taxes (1913)

Pensions (1914–26)

Step-up basis of capital gains at death (1921)

Lower rates on long-term capital gains (1921)

Deductibility of charitable contributions (1917)

$0 $50 $100 $150 $200

Billions (2010 Dollars)

Sources: Christopher Howard, *The Hidden Welfare State: Tax Expenditures and Social Policy in the United States* (Princeton, NJ: Princeton University Press, 1997), 176–77; Office of Management and Budget, *Analytical Perspectives, Budget of the United States Government, FY2011* (2010), http://www.gpoaccess.gov/usbudget/fy11/pdf/spec.pdf.

by employers, which is expected to cost $177 billion in 2011; it is followed by the Home Mortgage Interest Deduction, $104.5 billion; and the exclusion from taxes of employer-provided retirement benefits, $67.1 billion.[16] The number of such tax breaks continues to grow, and their purposes are varied, assisting Americans with everything from paying college tuition to purchasing energy-efficient windows and appliances to paying for child care. Their costs are substantial: on net, as of 2008, the amount lost in federal revenues due to social tax breaks was equivalent to 7.4 percent of GDP, up from 4.2 percent in 1976.[17] To put this in perspective, "visible governance," meaning total direct federal spending—on all domestic programs, the military, and interest on the debt—amounts to approximately 18 percent of GDP, making social tax expenditures comparable to between one-third and one-half as much.[18]

From an accounting perspective, direct social benefits and tax breaks both have the same effect: they impose costs on the federal budget, whether incurred in the form of obligations or lost revenues. As southern Democrat Russell Long, chair of the Senate Finance Committee from 1966 to 1981, said of the term "tax expenditures": "That label don't bother me. . . . I've never been confused about it. I've always known that what we're doing was giving government money away."[19] But for most beneficiaries, the experience is starkly different: those who receive direct benefits such as unemployment insurance or food stamps usually recognize that a government program assisted them, whereas few equate their lowered tax bills with comparable aid. Many Americans are unaware of how tax expenditures function, or even that they exist. For example, a poll in 2008, referring to what has become our most expensive social tax break, queried respondents about whether workers are required to pay taxes on the amounts their employers contribute to their health insurance benefits or not. Only half of the respondents, 50 percent, answered correctly by saying "no"; 29 percent mistakenly believed that people were required to pay such taxes, and 21 percent simply said they did not know.[20] In short, it is unsurprising that the energy Obama generated as a candidate evaporated once he turned to governance, for the agenda he pursued sought to transform policies that Americans barely know exist, and to create some new policies that they are unable to see.

Considering Governance from Citizens' Perspective

By Reagan's second term in office, scholars began to notice that traditional ways of thinking about government programs no longer reflected much of how public policies were actually designed and administered. In 1988 Donald Kettl depicted the new reality as "government by proxy," meaning "the provision of government goods and services through proxies such as contractors, grantees, and recipients of government tax breaks and loans."[21] In the years since, several scholars have elucidated these new forms of governance. Brinton Milward described the "hollow state," highlighting the "contracting out" of government services to nonprofits and for-profits; Christopher Howard revealed the political development of the "hidden welfare state" of tax expenditures; Jacob Hacker explained how government came to regulate and subsidize social benefits provided by private employers; Paul Light pointed to the "shadow of government," which emerges from the sum of these types of mechanisms; and Andrea Campbell and Kimberly Morgan detailed the workings of "delegated governance," meaning the allocation of authority for social welfare policy to nonstate actors.[22] Combined, these works and others make plain that increasingly government does not directly provide goods and services but operates instead through a variety of indirect mechanisms that permeate and structure aspects of the economy.

We have yet to learn, however, what ordinary Americans think of or even know about these ascendant forms of governance. We lack understanding of whether citizens support or oppose such policies, or—at a more basic level—whether they are aware of their existence and are thus able to form meaningful opinions about them. To the extent that such policies lack citizens' consent or approval, they may represent a fundamentally undemocratic development. We do not know how benefiting from them shapes citizens' views of government, of its legitimacy or of their obligations toward it. Neither do we know whether they prompt or discourage civic engagement, enabling citizens to mobilize and express their views to their representatives in the political system. A few scholars have theorized briefly that such policies are likely obscured from the view of most people, and thus probably fail to prompt citizens to take political action in relation to them.[23] Empirical evidence for or exploration of such claims, however, has yet to be offered.

Considering such policies from citizens' perspective, I have identified them, collectively, as the "submerged state," because that image conveys what amounts to their stealth presence in the lives of most Americans. The aim of this book is to investigate citizens' awareness and experiences of the submerged state, or their lack thereof; to explain the implications for reform efforts; and to consider how policymakers and citizens alike could take action to change these circumstances and to revitalize democracy.

The parameters of the concept of the submerged state deserve some clarification. The American propensity to place substantial amounts of government activity "out of sight," as historian Brian Balogh terms it, is not new; it has roots that run deep into the nineteenth century.[24] Over time, numerous social policies have been designed or altered to contain at least some submerged features or characteristics. Take Medicare, for instance: since the 1970s, Medicare beneficiaries have had the option of receiving their benefits through a private health insurance plan, and as of 2010, 24 percent of Medicare beneficiaries—11.1 million people—interacted not with government directly but rather with an insurance company, gaining benefits through what is called "Medicare Advantage."[25] The obvious confusion of the town meeting participant who told his congressman to "keep your government hands off my Medicare" may be less absurd than it appears if it emanated from the experience of public benefits that were actually delivered by the private sector.[26] In fact, in the United States, social programs in which benefits or services are provided directly by a government institution or agency are extremely rare. Consider, for example, that we do not require food stamps beneficiaries to shop at government-run food pantries, or Medicare patients to visit doctors only at government-run health clinics. It is appropriate, then, to think of all social programs as existing on a continuum from those that are most visible to those that are most submerged. The programs of the submerged state are distinctly clustered at one end of that spectrum, being especially camouflaged by their unique designs. Whereas some other policies possess features that may slightly obscure government's role, the policies of the submerged state do so far more completely, either by their placement in the tax code, through the subsidies or contracts with private organizations that deliver them, or both. It is these policies that are my focus here.

It should be noted, furthermore, that social welfare policy is but one of the many areas of contemporary governance in which the submerged state plays a prominent role. Other examples abound. For instance, subsidies to farmers have made some food products cheaper than others and influenced American consumption habits; the U.S. Department of Defense now hires private contractors to do many tasks that were previously reserved only for members of the armed forces; civil rights policies are structured to deal with racial and gender discrimination through private channels, encouraging litigation rather than bureaucratic regulation of business.[27] While any of these is worthy of investigation and likely compounds citizens' difficulties in perceiving what government does, my purview in this book is limited to policies geared to address households' economic security and well-being.

The Origins of the Submerged State

How did so much of U.S. governance come to be so heavily obscured from view? Policymakers built the foundation of the submerged state as we know it today during the early and mid-twentieth century, first largely by happenstance and then as a means of brokering political agreements. During the last thirty years of conservative governance, the submerged state has flourished. The composition of its policies has appealed to conservatives and liberals alike, such that in an era of increasingly sharp partisan divisions, it has offered a rare format for agreement on new policy initiatives. Also, some of the aggressive growth of the submerged state occurred automatically, as policies established long ago offered increasingly larger benefits due to changes such as the rise in housing values or health care costs—while political leaders looked the other way. As a result of both trends, the submerged state has expanded—even while some visible policies that aid poor and middle-income Americans atrophied. Since the 1970s, programs geared mostly for seniors, such as Social Security and Medicare, have remained strong, but various of those for younger people—for example, Pell Grants, unemployment insurance, and welfare—feature benefits that have deteriorated in value or coverage that has grown more restrictive.[28] On balance, in the lives of most Americans other than seniors, the impact of visible governance has diminished while that of the submerged state has grown.

Some of the earliest provisions of the submerged state either predated group mobilization in relevant domains or occurred beyond its radar screen. For example, when the framers of the original income tax code in 1913 opted to exclude mortgage interest from taxable income, they were not responding to group pressure. Rather, in omitting consumer debt from taxation, they followed a tradition that dated back to the Civil War period, while also seeking administrative simplicity that would aid in effective implementation.[29] During the 1910s and 1920s, policymakers enacted several other major social tax breaks, including the deduction of state and local taxes and charitable contributions.[30] Ironically, these components—minor footnotes early on—have ballooned to become vast entitlements today, and they are fiercely defended by the industries that benefit from them.

During the post–World War II period, innovations in the submerged state epitomized the fruit of political compromise. On some issues, policy enactment appears to have been possible only when the demands of vested interests were met through policy designs that accommodated them and thus prompted key moderate Democrats or Republicans to vote in favor of legislation.[31] For example, when the Johnson administration encountered steadfast opposition to student loan policy from bankers—more than from any other group—it finally invited a group of them to the White House to discuss the terms on which they would be willing to accept such a policy. These negotiations broke the logjam, leading to a final bill that included several features favorable to the banks in exchange for their support.[32]

In recent decades of conservative dominance and political polarization, the submerged state entered into its new stage of aggressive growth. Increasingly, the design of its policies became not a last resort but rather the template of choice for new policy initiatives. In an era when direct visible social policies have been under attack, submerged policies contain several attributes that have enabled them to overcome partisan divisions and institutional gridlock. They have gained favor for four reasons: first, Republicans and conservative Democrats find them attractive; second, other Democrats have proven willing to go along; third, institutional features of Congress make them easier to enact than new direct spending programs; and fourth, over time they have cultivated the support of interest groups that defend them vigorously.

The submerged state has long fused well with conservatives' political values and priorities. While hallmark programs of the visible state originated at the hands of mainstream Democrats, from the very beginning Republicans and a few conservative Democrats took the lead in submerged state-building. Christopher Howard reports that southern Democrats and conservative Republicans helped enact the income tax back in 1913, complete with its early tax expenditures, and in 1926 pro-business Republican Senator George McLean (R-CT) nonchalantly introduced the amendment that henceforth excluded employer pensions from taxation. In the early 1970s, Senator Russell Long judged President Richard Nixon's welfare reform plan to be too generous. He devised an alternative policy—the Earned Income Tax Credit (EITC)—that aimed to help the working poor through tax relief, and it passed easily as part of a larger tax bill in 1975.[33]

Conservatives' leadership in the construction of the submerged state is not accidental. All elected officials, if they wish to stay in office, need to find ways to represent citizens, to respond to the needs of those who elected them and those whose votes they would like to attract. The challenge for conservatives is doing this without expanding the visible state. Conservative politicians favor submerged state policies primarily because they enable them to deliver goods and services to core constituencies while neither creating vast new direct spending programs nor enlarging the federal bureaucracy in the process.

Submerged policies appeal to some contemporary conservatives because they can appear to restrain government spending. Tax expenditures, at first blush, might seem consistent with this goal because they reduce the amount government collects in revenues. Of course, in fact they do not reduce government obligations—they only limit the funds available to it for spending on other programs. But some policymakers assume that curtailing revenues provides a means by which to reduce spending, an approach that became known as "starve the beast." As articulated by Reagan in 1981: "Over the past decade we've talked about curtailing spending so that we can lower the tax burden. . . . But there were always those who told us that taxes couldn't be cut until spending was reduced. Well, you know, we can lecture our children about extravagance until we run out of voice and breath. Or we can cure their extravagance simply by reducing their allowance."[34] Some policymakers also believe that submerged policies, by bestowing rewards on some people, may quell popular demands for more extensive visible social provision for all citizens. Republican Senator Robert Packwood, chair of the Senate Finance Committee, implied this in 1983 when he defended the tax-free status of employer health insurance: "I think the one reason we do not have any significant demand for national health insurance in this country among those who are employed is because their employers are paying for their benefits, by and large. And we will never go to the situation in Great Britain so long as that system exists, and I hate to see us nibble at it for fear you are going to have the demand that the Federal Government take over and provide the benefits that would otherwise be lost."[35] The submerged state is thus supported in part because it is thought to deter direct government spending, both by reducing revenues and by appeasing those who might otherwise be vocal proponents.

Submerged state policies can also appear to embody the principle of privatization, meaning the contracting out of government responsibilities to the private sector on the assumption that it can deliver goods and services more efficiently. As such, they seem to reflect the kinds of market-based approaches that Reagan championed and that have become commonplace in American politics ever since his presidency. It is the case that the officials on the front lines of service delivery for such policies are not government bureaucrats but, instead, representatives of institutions such as health insurance companies and banks. Yet, in fact, such policies function not through free-market principles of laissez-faire but rather through public subsidization of the private sector. Some submerged policies, such as tax breaks, subsidize individuals to participate in activities that promote the profitability of particular industries; others, such as student loans, function by delivering public funds directly to the private sector. In either case, they encourage people to act differently than if they were left to pure market forces; for example, consumers are more likely to purchase bigger houses than they would if home-owner tax advantages did not exist, and this fuels the real estate industry. Nonetheless, these features of the submerged state help explain why conservatives have not acted to restrain even its policies that have grown to be hugely expensive, and why they have continued to initiate new ones.

Another critical factor that has enabled the submerged state to flourish in recent decades is that over time, a wider array of Democrats became willing accomplices—and leaders—in its creation. During the New Deal and Great Society periods, Democrats initiated the creation of new direct spending programs. When in the 1980s that approach to governance began to seem politically infeasible, they looked to the submerged state instead to find ways to aid low- and middle-income people. They increasingly acquiesced and supported policies such as tax expenditures because, to quote one member of Congress, they became "the only game in town."[36] After Democratic candidate Walter Mondale lost his bid for the presidency in 1984, the Democratic Leadership Council (DLC) formed in an effort to take control of the party away from liberals. The DLC championed tax expenditures, and in 1988 its affiliates in Congress pushed successfully for large increases in the EITC and for other new tax credits for the working poor.[37] While Republicans had proposed tuition tax breaks as far back as the early 1960s, it was Democratic President Bill Clinton who finally called for their successful enactment in the form of the HOPE and Lifetime Learning Tax Credits, which he signed into law. Once Democrats controlled both Congress and the White House in 2009, tax expenditures constituted their policy tool of choice, as numerous new and expanded tax breaks were tucked into bills intended to encourage particular activities and to stimulate the flagging economy.

With Congress so deeply and closely divided between the two major political parties in recent decades, submerged policies—particularly in the case of tax expenditures—have also proven easier to enact than other policies because the institutional hurdles are much lower. Direct new spending programs must overcome multiple hurdles in the budget process, gaining the approval of two separate committees in each chamber for authorization and appropriation. New tax breaks, by contrast, only need to pass muster with the tax committees, and they can be folded into large revenue bills, attracting little attention in floor votes.[38]

Over time, each well-established wing of the submerged state has been tended by the trade associations and other interest groups that represent its core industries—such as the National Association of Realtors and National Association of Home Builders in the case of the Home Mortgage Interest Deduction (HMID). Such groups have carefully cultivated and tended relationships with elected officials on both sides of the aisle. They have long made their positions known through lobbying in Washington, D.C., and by activating their constituencies; in recent decades, as the cost of campaigns has escalated, they have devoted substantial amounts to donations. Such influence serves as another important reason why substantial components of the submerged state enjoy strong bipartisan support, resilient enough to withstand the sharp partisan divisions around most other issues.

In short, over the past thirty years, by nurturing and protecting the submerged state, conservatives did not downsize government; rather, they took the lead in restructuring and actually enlarging it, but in ways that elude the public. Liberals, with few alternatives, willingly followed suit. Meanwhile interest groups worked to maintain strong support for their favored policies from members of both parties.

The Size and Scope of the Submerged State

As a result of these attributes, submerged state policies of many varieties have proliferated in number and in scope during the conservative period of the past three decades. To illustrate such trends, this section will focus on social tax expenditures. When Reagan took office in 1981, 81 of these existed; by 2010, Obama's second year in office, the number had risen by 86 percent, to 151. The number of such policies increased steadily but slowly during the 1980s and 1990s, then grew more rapidly from 2000 to the present—both when Republicans controlled both chambers of Congress and the White House and more recently when Democrats did.[39]

The amount of total revenue lost to social tax expenditures soared between 1981 and 2010, in 2010 dollars, as shown in figure 1.3. The temporary decline in the late 1980s is attributable primarily to the effect of tax reform in 1986. It is important to note that even in this major legislation policymakers treated social tax expenditures as sacrosanct, leaving intact all of the most costly ones. The reason why their overall value dipped was because tax reform lowered regular tax rates, and when households owe less, the worth of individual tax breaks is effectively reduced.[40] Nonetheless, after a few years of stasis, the actual cost of tax breaks began to grow

FIGURE 1.3. Revenue Lost from All Social Tax Expenditures, 1981–2010 (2010 Dollars)

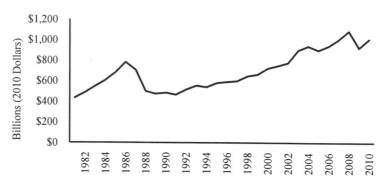

Sources: Joint Committee on Taxation, "Estimates of Federal Tax Expenditures for Fiscal Years" (various years), http://www.jct.gov/publications.html; Congressional Budget Office, "Tax Expenditures: Current Issues and Five-Year Budget Projections for Fiscal Years 1982–1986" (1981), http://www.cbo.gov/ftpdocs/51xx/doc5185/doc29-Entire.pdf.

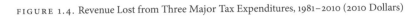

FIGURE 1.4. Revenue Lost from Three Major Tax Expenditures, 1981–2010 (2010 Dollars)

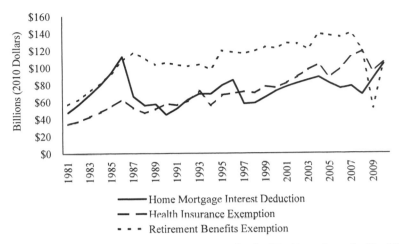

Sources: Joint Committee on Taxation, "Estimates of Federal Tax Expenditures for Fiscal Years" (various years), http://www.jct.gov/publications.html; Congressional Budget Office, "Tax Expenditures: Current Issues and Five-Year Budget Projections for Fiscal Years 1982–1986" (1981), http://www.cbo.gov/ftpdocs/51xx/doc5185/doc29-Entire.pdf.

steadily and rapidly again, increasing by more than 130 percent by 2008.[41] In that year, just before the recession temporarily reduced their value, they cost the nation $1.086 trillion, and recently their cost has nearly returned to that level.

The three most expensive social tax expenditures were each created long ago—starting with the case of the Home Mortgage Interest Deduction in 1913—and have expanded tremendously in terms of their value in recent decades. Figure 1.4 shows the value, in 2010 dollars, of the HMID, and the nontaxable status of health insurance and retirement benefits. Notably, while each diminished briefly in the late 1980s and early 1990s for the reasons mentioned above, they then once again resumed their growth, which was mitigated only briefly by the recession in 2008.

Their low profile notwithstanding, submerged state policies consume a large portion of federal resources relative to many social programs that are more much more visible. Figure 1.5 shows the size of the three most expensive social tax expenditures compared to the value of a few well-known direct social programs. The HMID consumes four times the amount of the primary federal housing program for low-income Americans, called Section 8 Housing vouchers. Despite the amount of attention often given in public discourse to welfare (now called Temporary Assistance for Needy

FIGURE 1.5. Selected Visible and Submerged Social Expenditures, 2007 (2010 Dollars)

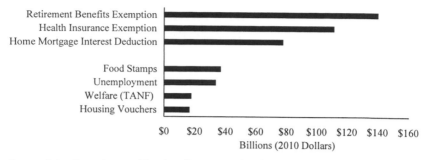

Sources: Joint Committee on Taxation, "Estimates of Federal Tax Expenditures, 2007–2011" (2007), http://www.jct.gov/publications.html?func=startdown&id=1198; Office of Management and Budget, *Analytical Perspectives: Budget of the United States Government FY 2009* (2008), tables 3.2, 8.5, http://www.gpoaccess.gov/usbudget/fy09/pdf/spec.pdf; Congressional Budget Office, Budget Factsheets for TANF, Food Stamps, and Unemployment (March 2007).

Families), it costs the nation less than one-fifth the amount of subsidizing employer-provided health insurance and less than one-seventh the expense of employer-provided retirement benefits. Neither the costs of food stamps, the most utilized program for low-income people, nor of unemployment insurance, which provides economic security for Americans of all income levels, amounts to as much as half the value of even the least expensive of these programs.

Fostering Economic Inequality

Because the submerged state typically distributes its rewards through more complex and circuitous processes than do more direct policies, its major beneficiaries are often not obvious. To the extent that lawmakers discuss the submerged state publicly, they usually imply that its policies facilitate widely held goals, such as the expansion of health care coverage or growth of retirement savings for average citizens. In some instances, such images are reasonably accurate depictions of policy effects, as exemplified by the Earned Income Tax Credit, which subsidizes the earnings of the working poor, or the tuition tax credits signed into law by Clinton, which aided middle-income Americans in paying for college. Most submerged policies, however, actually exacerbate inequality: they shower their most generous benefits on affluent people, and they generate detrimental side effects that adversely impact those who are less well-off. Some of the largest winnings, moreover, are accrued not by individuals and households but rather by the third-party organizations and businesses that benefit from the economic activities such policies promote.

Figure 1.6 illustrates how the three most costly tax expenditures distribute their benefits across income groups. Each bestows its bounty in an upwardly redistributive fashion, with the largest amounts going to those in the upper-income groups. The most skewed distribution accompanies the Home Mortgage Interest Deduction and the tax-free status of retirement benefits: in 2004, 69 percent and 55 percent of the benefits from each of these policies, respectively, were conferred on Americans with household incomes of $100,000 or more—the top 15 percent of the income distribution.[42] The tax-free nature of employer-sponsored health insurance is somewhat less biased, though still 30 percent of the benefit was allocated to families in the top 15 percent of the income distribution.

On the rare occasions when policymakers ever talk about the Home Mortgage Interest Deduction, they typically convey the impression that it helps make home-ownership possible for middle-income people. Scholars

FIGURE 1.6. Percent of Tax Subsidies Claimed by Households, by Income, 2004

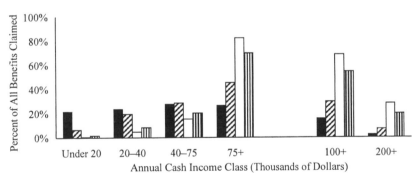

Sources: Leonard E. Burman et al., "Tax Code, Employer-Sponsored Insurance, and Tax Subsidies," in *Using Taxes to Reform Health Insurance*, edited by Leonard E. Burman and Henry J. Aaron (Washington, DC: Brookings Institution Press, 2008); Joint Committee on Taxation, "Estimates of Federal Tax Expenditures for Fiscal Years 2005–2009" (2005), http://www.jct.gov/publications.html?func=startdown&id=1200; Leonard E. Burman et al., "Distributional Effects of Defined Contribution Plans and Individual Retirement Accounts," Tax Policy Center Discussion paper No. 16 (2004), http://www.urban.org/uploadedPDF/311029 TPC DP16.pdf.

have not found evidence to support this effect, however; rather the policy merely offers an extra financial advantage to those who were already positioned to buy a home.[43] HMID offers particularly generous aid, as we have seen, to the wealthy. Whereas the median new home value in the nation has fluctuated between $200,000 and $260,000 since 2006, the HMID applies to mortgages up to $1,000,000; those who can afford to buy the most expensive homes and qualify for the largest mortgages reap by far the largest benefits from the policy.[44] Moreover, both the HMID and other benefits for home owners operate as artificial incentives that encourage people to purchase more expensive and larger homes than they would in their absence. As a result, such policies inflate prices, making home-ownership more out-of-reach for non-owners. For those who are financially capable of buying a home, housing equity provides their primary source of wealth, and that further widens the economic gap between owners and renters. In addition, the lost government revenues leave lawmakers with insufficient funds to maintain or create policies that could more effectively enhance the social welfare of low- and moderate-income citizens.[45]

The employer-provided and government-subsidized benefits of the submerged state are also tilted to higher-income Americans and have become more so over time. During the 1940s, increasing numbers of jobs offered workers such benefits, and before long, the majority of Americans enjoyed coverage. As health care costs soared in recent years, however, fewer and fewer jobs granted health coverage to employees: the percentage of Americans possessing it diminished in every consecutive year from 2000 to 2009, falling from 68 to 59 percent over the period.[46] In addition, the extent of the plans that are still offered by employers has diminished.[47] While higher-income people have long been most likely to gain employment in positions that offer health insurance and have had the good fortune of being covered by more generous plans, the inequality fostered by such arrangements has become exacerbated recently. As of 2009, in the lowest income quintile, only 16 percent of Americans under age sixty-five had employer-sponsored health insurance—compared to 85 percent of those in the top quintile; while rates of coverage had declined among all quintiles, they had fallen most precipitously for those at and near the bottom.[48] In addition, even among those who do have such coverage, the value of the tax subsidies is sharply skewed to the wealthy: the average subsidy for households with incomes between $200,000 and $500,000 is over three times the average subsidy for those in the $10,000 to $20,000 range, $4,791 compared to $1,535.[49] As a result, this large portion of the submerged state, which not many Americans realize is subsidized by government, showers its benefits far more generously on the haves than on the have-nots.

Well beyond its impact on individuals and families, the submerged state exacerbates economic inequality by promoting some entire sectors of the economy over others, at government expense. In delivering subsidies to particular industries and creating incentives for people to participate in specific market activities, its policies protect and enhance profit-making capabilities in those areas. From 1980 until the current recession, the core sectors that it nurtures—finance, insurance, and real estate—outpaced growth in other sectors of the American economy.[50] The fortunes of these industries emanated not from "market forces" alone but rather from their interplay with the hidden policies that promoted their growth and heaped extra benefits on them.

Such patterns are exemplified by the rise in profitability of the student loan sector. Americans' need for student aid escalated during the 1980s and 1990s as the rise in tuition rates exceeded inflation. Amid the growing partisan divide in Congress, policymakers could forge agreement more easily on terms for student loans, for which they needed to do little more than expand borrowing limits and loosen eligibility requirements, than they could on Pell Grants, the direct form of tuition assistance for low-income students, for which rate increases would have involved the highly conflictual and many-staged process of legislative approval for increased spending.[51] As a result of these trends, growing numbers of students borrowed, the average amount of their loans soared, and lending became increasingly lucrative. Student lender Sallie Mae, created by the federal government in 1973 and permitted to become a private company in 1996, saw the value of its stocks rise by nearly 2000 percent over the next decade, compared to the Standard and Poor 500's average gain of 228 percent. Its CEO became the most highly compensated in the nation, with approximately $37 million in salary, bonuses, and stock awards in 2006.[52]

Similarly, government subsidies for health insurance appeared more complicit in the development of the "winner take all" society than in providing for the health care of the nation's citizens. Health insurance companies enjoyed soaring profits that did not abate even with the recession: the five largest insurers reported $12.2 billion in profits in 2009, a 56 percent increase from 2008.[53] For the CEOs of the top seven health insurance companies, average total compensation, including stock options, soared to $10.6 million.[54] Meanwhile, among ordinary Americans, the ranks of the uninsured escalated, reaching 16.7 percent in 2010, and the insured faced mounting costs.[55]

Whereas most Americans assume social welfare policy exists in order to provide economic security to average people and to lessen inequality, the policies of the submerged state have aided and abetted the upward distribution of riches, with more and more of the largesse accrued to those at the very top. The sectors that it nurtures, in turn, have invested in strengthening their political capacity, fortifying their ability to defend existing arrangements.

Undermining Citizenship

While the submerged state has showered benefits especially on affluent families and powerful industries, most Americans have gained little from it, and they are barely aware of its existence. It functions largely without their knowledge or consent. As such, the submerged state threatens to undermine the basic principles encapsulated in the idea of "government of the people, by the people, for the people." When government is invisible, it is no surprise that people feel they cannot trust it and that it is ineffective. If citizens witness clearly the activities of powerful interest groups but cannot perceive government making a difference in their own lives or those of their families, neighbors, or communities, it makes sense if they conclude that it is not responsive to them. Submerging the state does not foster citizenship: it inculcates passivity and resentment.

Democracy depends, first of all, on citizens having the means and capacity to form meaningful opinions about acts of governance. The submerged state interferes with that process, for how can citizens establish their own views about its policies—opinions that reflect their values and interests—if they have only limited or faulty information about those policies, or have never even heard of them? The fact that some citizens are not aware that Medicare, a relatively visible program that has only some submerged features, emanates from government—as epitomized by the exchange between a congressman and constituent reported in this book's introduction—underscores the problems generated by programs that are fully embedded in the submerged state.

The submerged state conducts governance by "smoke and mirrors": to unsuspecting citizens, its policies may appear to embody genuine reductions in government spending and to embrace market principles, but in fact both impressions misconstrue reality. As Eugene Steuerle, a tax economist at the Urban Institute, said of the differences between tax expenditures and direct government programs: "One looks like smaller government; one looks like bigger government. In fact, they both do exactly the same thing."[56] The confusing composition of the submerged state likely confounds citizens, blinding them to its size, growth, and upwardly distributive effects—if not to its very existence. Without basic information about its policies, citizens are ill-positioned to form and articulate opinions about them, or even to understand what is at stake in reform efforts such as those launched by Obama. More broadly, they are likely to assume that markets are more autonomous and effective than they are in actuality, and they may well fail to give government due credit for addressing society's problems.

Beyond opinion formation, vibrant democracy requires that citizens possess the inclination and capacity to take action, to exercise their political voice in order to express their views. Scholars have found that some direct and visible policies have the potential to enhance individuals' interest in politics, their sense that government is responsive to people like them, and their disposition to become involved. Some do this directly through the resources they bestow on recipients, for example, by elevating their level of education, which in turn develops their skills for political involvement and places them in social networks in which they are more likely to be recruited to participate. Others do so by conveying messages to citizens through their experience of program benefits and delivery: they may learn that government is responsive to people like them, for instance, or that they are valued citizens, and thus become more willing to participate. Owing to such dynamics, low- and moderate-income recipients of both Social Security and the G.I. Bill participated in politics at higher levels than would have been expected on the basis of their socioeconomic characteristics alone.[57]

By contrast, if individuals benefit from policies without knowing they emanate from government, as in the case of submerged state policies, that experience is unlikely to offer the kinds of cognitive effects associated with the receipt of other policies. Veterans who used the G.I. Bill to acquire education or training after World War II were plainly aware that government financed the policy. "Thank God the government had the doors open for us," said one veteran who pursued vocational training and became a custom builder.[58] Contrast his reaction with that of the student loan beneficiary mentioned earlier, who doubted that he had actually used a government program.

People cannot be expected to take action to advocate for or express opposition to policies of which they are scarcely aware. If program recipients themselves are largely oblivious, the general public will be more so; the submerged state does little to engage either as policy advocates. Conversely, the rich resources that the submerged state bestows on privileged industries fosters their political involvement—in the form of campaign contributions and interest group lobbying. As such, it exacerbates the political voices of the rich and powerful, making them more audible than those of ordinary Americans. These political dynamics are more characteristic of oligarchy, the rule by the few, than of democracy. They also illuminate why the submerged state has been so resistant to change.

From *Nudge* to Reveal

The transformation of public policies so that they distribute resources fairly to Americans across the income spectrum and accomplish widely held goals cannot be achieved simply through the force of dynamic personalities or lofty principles. Rather, reform-minded leaders must confront the existing policies of the submerged state and fundamentally alter them, if not dismantle them. It is a profoundly challenging task that harkens back to state-building efforts in the Progressive Era of the early twentieth century. As explained by Stephen Skowronek, drawing on what his analysis of that era revealed about reform generally, "Success hinges on recasting official power relationships within governmental institutions and altering ongoing relations between state and society."[59] In our time, the transformation of the submerged state requires, first of all, the reconstitution of deeply established relationships between powerful economic actors and their allies in the political system.

Obama encountered head-on an existing state that is at once formidable and elusive, and thus the quest to accomplish his agenda for social policy required engagement in treacherous political battles. In the process, he took on entrenched beneficiaries of submerged policies. Remarkably, he did manage to claim victory over the student loan companies, and to extract agreement and cooperation from powerful health care industries in the process of reform. His efforts to scale back the upwardly distributive effects of social tax expenditures, by contrast, have been largely defeated as business and organizational beneficiaries forced him to beat a hasty retreat. Meanwhile the public, in whose name these battles have been fought, has barely offered more than tepid support even for key victories. In fact, after signing major legislation, the president had to try to convince the public of the value of what his administration has accomplished. Legislative achievements remain unstable and prone to being dismantled by opponents.

The daunting politics of the submerged state—highly aware and energized interest groups, unchecked by the public, which remains passive and oblivious—need not, however, be inevitable. The central questions I ask in this book are, Why is reform of the submerged state so challenging, and how can it be carried out successfully and legislative accomplishments secured? The pursuit of answers to these questions endorses a general principal embraced by the Obama administration: to follow the lead of social science research, including that which is experimental in nature and which examines how aspects of policy design and delivery influence human behavior. But while applauding the particular scholarly approach that Obama has embraced as far as it goes, I aim to expand its purview—to consider how policies affect citizens' awareness and understanding of government.

Where Roosevelt drew on his "Brains Trust," a group of law professors who influenced the shape of the New Deal, and Clinton relied on the ideas of economist Robert Reich and political theorist Bill Galston, Obama has surrounded himself with proponents of behavioral economics. This approach, which has gained momentum over the past fifteen years, brings insights from psychology to bear on economic analysis. Its advocates within the administration have included Cass Sunstein, the coauthor of the popular behavioral economics manifesto *Nudge*, as head of the Office of Information and Regulatory Affairs; Jeff Liebman of Harvard, who served as deputy to the budget director; Austan Goolsbee of the University of Chicago, chairman of the Council of Economic Advisers; and Alan Krueger of Princeton University as assistant secretary for Economic Policy and Michael Barr, assistant secretary for Financial Institutions, both of the Treasury Department.[60]

Behavioral economists champion experimental research, conducted with the rigor of randomized drug trials, to determine which policies work and which do not. Rather than introducing grand new theories about governance, they have sought to fine-tune the details, aiming to make governance more effective. Identifying systematic ways that people fail to act in their own interests, they seek policies designed to encourage them to do so. They favor such plans, for example, as automatic enrollments in pensions for workers without a 401(k), making the terms on credit cards easier for people to understand, and sending households without itemized deductions copies of completed tax forms that they only need to sign and return.[61] Their approach is thus highly useful in shaping public policy to promote the attainment of salutary social and economic goals, such as saving for retirement and healthier eating habits.

While the attributes of behavioral economics, including its nonpartisanship, are therefore commendable, the approach circumvents the core ambitions that Obama prioritized in his campaign, namely, restoring the connection between Americans and their government and revitalizing citizenship. Put differently, its goals neglect the central purpose of American governance, which is democracy itself. Its proponents favor using policy to encourage people to spend their money in all sorts of worthy ways, such as to stimulate the economy, to purchase health insurance, or to buy energy-saving appliances. These ambitions regard people primarily as consumers, as participants in markets, who need choices arranged for them in strategic ways so they will be induced to behave appropriately. Fundamental to democracy, by contrast, is the idea that people are citizens, active participants in governance. It requires that people should be reasonably aware of what representatives do on their behalf; that they should be able to form their own views about such actions; and that they should have the capacity for involvement in the political process, to have their voices heard. Policy analysts need to consider, then, how public policies influence the health of democracy.

I contend that the hallmark of behavioral economics—evidence-based policymaking—can be extended and applied to restoring the connection between government and citizens. Featuring research that puts such concerns front and center, this book argues that democratic governance and vibrant citizenship require policymakers to "reveal" the operation of policies—their existence and basic impact. It turns the spotlight to how policies affect civic life—influencing citizens' understanding of policies and their attitudes about government. Survey research and experiments enable us to examine questions such as which kinds of policy designs make the workings of government evident to citizens; how citizens can be informed about policies such that they can form opinions about them; and what kinds of information permit them to establish views in keeping with their values and interests. By shifting the goal from "nudging" people to make sound choices as consumers to "revealing" governance to citizens, we can begin to revitalize democracy.

2 · THE POLITICS OF THE SUBMERGED STATE

"People came out of the woodwork for Obama during the campaign, but now they are hibernating," said Lynda Smith of Iowa, as she explained the challenges of generating grassroots support for health care reform in the summer of 2009. Smith, who retired from her factory job and took a position as a greeter at Walmart, had volunteered during 2008 first on Hillary Clinton's campaign and then on Barack Obama's. She continued to try to promote the president's agenda once he was elected but found she had little company. Similarly, fellow Iowan Bonnie Adkins held a highly publicized potluck supper at her home, an event for local Democrats to come and make calls to build support for the president's top policy priority, but only ten people showed up. "The enthusiasm is not there like it was a year ago," she commented.[1]

But while ordinary Americans who had supported a reform agenda receded from involvement, interest groups with a stake in the outcome intensified their already high levels of activism. During the 2008 campaign season, the health care sector—including doctors' associations, drug companies, and HMOs—had contributed $167.3 million, either by donating directly to political candidates or by channeling funds through party committees. In 2009 they devoted their efforts to lobbying elected officials. Trade associations representing the industry had steadily increased their spending on lobbying, funneling $3.4 billion to that purpose since 1998. In 2009 Pharmaceutical Research and Manufacturers of America—known as "PhRMA"—ranked as the top spender on lobbying in the health care sector, paying $26 million to share their ideas with lawmakers; other drug companies—namely, Pfizer, Amgen, and Eli Lilly—followed close behind. Many other types of organizations outside of the health care sector also lobbied on health care policy, including the Chamber of Commerce: its $144 million dwarfed the spending of all other groups and more than doubled its 2008 spending of $62 million.[2] The public might have returned to its slumber after Election Day, but organized interests with a stake in the submerged state made their presence known with a roar in the nation's capital.

Efforts to reform the submerged state routinely elicit sharp disparities in the level of participation, interest, and attention exhibited by interest groups compared to the public, even activists within it. Parallel observations about energized groups versus a passive public are often made about many areas of American politics, but the submerged state is striking in the extent to which the policies themselves play a role in fostering such outcomes. Over the course of their existence, the obscured policies of this area of governance have evolved to become illustrative cases of a phenomenon first highlighted long ago by political scientist E. E. Schattschneider: "New policies create a new politics."[3] Our inquiry here follows the more recent lead of Paul Pierson, who directed attention specifically to how policies, once established, yield what are called "policy feedback effects," influencing the political behavior of interest groups and mass publics.[4] Examining both in tandem reveals that the politics engendered by the submerged state are habitually imbalanced. Its policies inculcate in interest groups a steadfast attention to the issues, the habit of staying in touch with elected officials year in and year out, and readiness to mobilize when the provisions they favor are under attack. By contrast, these same policies leave much of the public, even beneficiaries themselves, unaware of government's role, incognizant of how the policies function or of what is at stake in reform efforts, and unengaged and unlikely to take action. Trends over the past fifteen years have exacerbated these inequities in the political voice of entrenched interests and the general public, making reform efforts all the more challenging and costly, both in financial and political terms.

Energizing Organized Interests

As the submerged state developed over the past century, interest groups became increasingly supportive of its presence, even if they had been less than enthusiastic at the inception of key policies. In some instances early on, groups paid little attention to policy developments, as in the initial creation of the income tax code. More often, they fought new policies vehemently, leaving reform-minded public officials little choice but to create policies that accommodated them by granting them expensive subsidies and incentives as a reward for going along. This latter pattern, which sociologists Paul Starr and Gosta Esping-Andersen termed "passive intervention," occurred repeatedly in the areas of housing and health care reform.[5]

Over time, particularly as they won favored modifications of policies, trade associations and other industry groups found that such policies served their interests well, and they became their most ardent defenders. For example, home builders' and realtors' associations paid little attention to the long-standing tax breaks for home-ownership until, in the late 1960s, Congress began to publish a list of them with the annual budget. Thereafter, such groups mobilized politically to protect the provisions, sending their lobbyists to Capitol Hill and activating their members around the country to pressure elected officials. Political scientist Christopher Howard observes that such activism paid off: "Between 1967 and 1995, the total cost of the home mortgage interest deduction increased by an average of almost 7 percent per year, adjusted for inflation."[6] Similarly, bankers had opposed the passage of student loan policy in 1965, but by 1993 became its fierce advocates. When the Clinton administration proposed replacing the existing system with direct lending, thus terminating lender subsidies, banks, lenders, and their trade associations led the fight to preserve the arrangements on which they had come to rely.[7] Before long, each component of the submerged state acquired its own powerful interest group allies. The strong relationships forged between these groups and political actors served the mutual interests of both.

Over the past two decades, these relationships between political actors and interest groups intensified, evolving from interdependence to interpenetration. This occurred in a political context in which the amounts of money invested in American politics—both in campaign spending and on lobbying—skyrocketed in real terms. The trend away from labor-intensive political campaigns to capital-intensive ones is hardly new, but it has been exacerbated in recent decades. Between 1990 and 2006, the average amount spent by winners of House elections nearly doubled, growing from $697,205 to $1,362,239 in 2008 dollars; spending by the average Senate winner rose by about 75 percent, from $5,433,276 in 1990 to $9,435,839 in 2006, in 2008 dollars.[8] Meanwhile, affluent individuals poured more money into campaigns through "soft money" contributions—funds spent to influence electoral outcomes but not channeled directly to candidates.[9] Nonprofit groups that serve as the conduit for such funds, called "527s" owing to their identification in the tax code, proliferated.[10] Meanwhile, the overall amount spent on lobbying increased by 90 percent in real terms between 1999 and 2009, growing from $1.93 billion to $3.55 billion, in 2010 dollars.

As the amount of money in politics escalated, the industries aided by

the presence of the submerged state—finance, real estate, and insurance—
enjoyed soaring profits that vastly outpaced those in other sectors, and
thus they became poised to invest more heavily in enhancing their political capacity to protect the policies that had served them so well. Their sector poured vast resources into campaign contributions and lobbying, out-
spending all others in both domains and rapidly increasing such spending
over time. Figure 2.1 shows total campaign contributions over time in three
specific industries that have benefited greatly from the submerged state.
Among them, real estate was by far the biggest spender, and it increased
its contributions from $43 million in the 1992 presidential election to $138
million in 2008, in 2010 dollars (see right-hand y-axis). As one indicator
of the health care industry, the health services component shown here
includes health maintenance organizations and managed care organizations such as Aetna and BlueCross BlueShield, and some other providers;
it should be noted that this does not include doctors or other health professionals, drug companies, or hospitals. Though campaign contributions
by the health services industry were much smaller than those of the real
estate industry, they increased at a slightly faster rate, quadrupling between 1992 and 2008, and student lenders meanwhile elevated their contributions by an impressive 350 percent (see left-hand y-axis).

The amounts these same industries spent on lobbying catapulted between 1998 and 2009, as shown in figure 2.2. Lobbyists for trade associations representing student lenders found themselves constantly pursued

FIGURE 2.1. Campaign Contributions, Selected Industries, 1990–2008

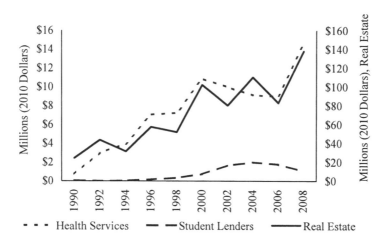

Source: Center for Responsive Politics, "Interest Groups," OpenSecrets.org, http://www.opensecrets
.org/industries/index.php.

FIGURE 2.2. Lobbying Spending, Selected Industries, 1998–2009

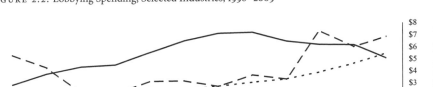

Source: Center for Responsive Politics, "Interest Groups," OpenSecrets.org, http://www.opensecrets.org/industries/index.php.

by politicians asking them to attend fund-raising receptions or to pledge their financial commitment to their campaigns.[11] The lenders' increase in spending over the period—27 percent in real terms (see right-hand y-axis)—was dwarfed, however, by a rise of 73 percent by real estate, and fully 186 percent by the health services industry (see left-hand y-axis).

While these organizations representing powerful interests in the submerged state have amplified their political voice over time, few organizations represent the views of the general public on such matters. Since the 1970s, the large broad-based membership groups that previously served to articulate the preferences of the general public have dwindled in size. In national politics, though the number of citizens' organizations has proliferated, the grassroots groups have been replaced by advocacy organizations without a membership base and thus lacking comparable organizing capacity and political effectiveness.[12] Moreover, unlike visible policies that more readily attract group loyalty, policies of the submerged state are typically too hidden and their status too unclear to generate such affiliations.[13] Historically, some broad-based membership organizations—namely, unions and the AARP—sometimes made compromises that positioned them as either defenders of existing arrangements or as less-than-ardent advocates for reform.[14] By 2009 these organizations came on board in support of health care reform and offered a strong countervailing force to the power of the industries, but in other issue areas involving the submerged state, such voices were either absent or very small.

People often assume that the interest groups representing powerful industries are rigidly partisan, but this tends not to be the case. For a decade beginning in the mid-1990s, congressional Republicans pursued what was called the "K Street strategy," striving to promote loyalty in staffing and campaign donating by the groups whose interests they chose to serve.[15] Yet such organizations deftly avoided forming exclusive partisan relationships and maintained instead what has been their traditional multi-pronged, bi-partisan approach.[16] Their political strategies are threefold. First, they strive to maintain and strengthen close relationships with elected officials who are particularly inclined to support them—predominantly Republicans and also some Democrats—by providing them with information, hearing their ideas, and ensuring that they will exert the energy to represent them effectively.[17] Second, on issues characterized by a rigid partisan divide, interest groups often focus on converting a few individuals to vote for their favored position. Although political scientists have usually found little evidence for such effects,[18] nonetheless their frequency need not be great in order to alter outcomes; in 2010 just destabilizing one senator's support for an issue could be enough to thwart legislative action. Third, interest groups seek to cultivate cordial relationships with candidates and elected officials and candidates on both "sides of the aisle." This is evidenced by the fact that their campaign contributions are typically distributed widely to both parties, with a slight edge to the party holding or expected to win the majority. Such patterns may help explain why even in a highly partisan environment, on some issues—as we will see—industries have been able to count on support from both Republicans and Democrats.

In sum, over time the policies of the submerged state have reshaped the political power of interest groups in ways that present profound challenges to reformers and imperil the success of the legislative achievements they manage to win. As the wealth of the industries they represented expanded in tandem with the stakes of their political involvement, such organizations invested enormous resources in attempting to influence the political process. The Obama administration thus confronted highly sophisticated efforts to protect the status quo. As a result, reform has required either defeating entrenched interests—which has proven impossible in most cases—or, more typically, negotiating with and accommodating them, which hardly appears to be the kind of change Obama's supporters expected when he won office. Yet whereas the submerged state fosters highly mobilized groups that represent the industries it benefits, it renders the public complacent, as we will now see.

Promoting Passive Mass Publics

Vigorous citizen involvement and electoral turnout during the 2008 presidential campaign helped usher Obama into office, but after his inauguration supportive mass publics withdrew. Fledgling efforts to mobilize Americans who favored his policy agenda were coordinated by a few groups, including the new grassroots component of the Democratic National Committee, Organizing for America; Health Care for America NOW!—a coalition of several unions; MoveOn.org; and Planned Parenthood. Yet the most evident popular momentum emerged among conservative opponents—particularly the insurgent Tea Party. The shortage of vocal support for the president's agenda is not surprising because in taking on the submerged state, Obama engaged in a set of battles over policies that are obscure, if not invisible, to much of the public.[19]

Influencing Policy Awareness

Policies of the submerged state do little to instill in their beneficiaries an awareness that they have utilized public social benefits. In a national survey conducted in 2008, the Social and Governmental Issues and Participation Study (hereafter, Governmental Issues Survey), respondents were asked up front whether they had "ever used a government social program, or not."[20] In answering this question, 43.5 percent of respondents replied in the affirmative, saying they had ever used a government social program, and 56.5 percent said they had never used one. Later they were asked whether they had ever benefited personally from any of nineteen specific federal social policies, including some that belong to the submerged state and others that are visible and direct in their design and delivery. In contrast to answers to the general question about social program usage, 91.6 percent of all respondents confirmed that they had used at least one of these programs at some point in their lives.

Table 2.1 presents the percentage of beneficiaries of each policy who reported at the outset that they had never used a government social program. Notably, the six italicized policies that head the list are precisely those belonging to the submerged state: tax-deferred savings accounts (529s and Coverdells), several tax expenditures, and student loans. The majority of beneficiaries of five of these policies and a near majority of the sixth—the Earned Income Tax Credit—failed to acknowledge government social program usage.

The unlikelihood of these submerged state beneficiaries to respond affirmatively does not appear to emanate from differences in the average size of their program benefits but rather from the design and the style of their delivery. This is evidenced by a study that compared, across time up through 2000, the average benefit rate in several of these policies in 2002 dollars. The

TABLE 2.1. Percentage of Beneficiaries of Specific Programs Who Report that They "Have Not Used a Government Social Program"

Program	"No, Have Not Used a Government Social Program" (%)
529 or Coverdell Tax-Deferred Savings	64.3
Home Mortgage Interest Deduction	60.0
HOPE or Lifetime Learning Tax Credit	59.6
Student Loans	53.3
Child and Dependent Care Tax Credit	51.7
Earned Income Tax Credit	47.1
Social Security—Retirement and Survivors	44.1
Pell Grants	43.1
Unemployment Insurance	43.0
Veterans Benefits (other than G.I. Bill)	41.7
G.I. Bill	40.3
Medicare	39.8
Head Start	37.2
Social Security Disability	28.7
SSI—Supplemental Security Income	28.2
Medicaid	27.8
Welfare/Public Assistance	27.4
Government Subsidized Housing	27.4
Food Stamps	25.4

Note: Submerged state policies shown in italics. $N = 1,370$.

Source: Social and Governmental Issues and Participation Study, 2008.

program in table 2.1 that comes to mind most readily for beneficiaries as emanating from government—food stamps—was worth at most $1,728 per year, and that was in 1981; its real value declined after that time such that by 2000 it was worth only $1,092. Average annual benefits for programs of the submerged state were considerably more generous. For instance, the average beneficiary of the Home Mortgage Interest Deduction received a benefit of $2,406 when it peaked in 1996, and of the Earned Income Tax Credit, $2,023 in 2000.[21] The average student loan beneficiary borrowed $4,725 annually in 2000, at a low rate of interest subsidized by government.[22] Despite the size of such benefits, many of those who utilized them failed to recognize them as coming from government social programs.

This is regardless of the fact that beneficiaries of submerged state policies clearly regarded the provisions to be valuable. Many recipients of tax breaks—often large majorities—reported that the policies they utilized were of help to them. For example, among HMID users, 37 percent claimed that it helped "a great deal," and 36 percent said "to some extent";

only 25 percent answered that it helped only "a little," and 2 percent volunteered "not at all."[23] Yet despite the size of their benefits and the fact that most beneficiaries found them quite helpful, recipients simply failed to think of them as social benefits emanating from government.

A conceptual issue discussed in the previous chapter is made evident by table 2.1: that in terms of their visibility to citizens, policies appear to fall along a continuum from most visible to most submerged, rather than merely clustering at two poles. Even in the case of some policies that operate neither through the tax system nor as private subsidies, particular design features seem to mask government's role in the perception of a large share of beneficiaries. Surprisingly, for example, only 44 percent of Social Security beneficiaries perceive themselves to have benefited from a government social program. This is despite the large size of the benefits: in 2000 the average Social Security beneficiary received $9,648 (in 2002 dollars) if making claims as an individual retired worker, and $20,064 if he or she had been widowed by a worker and had two children.[24] And program invisibility hardly seems related to the form of delivery: Social Security benefits arrive in the seemingly unambiguous form of checks from the government. Their submerged character for many recipients can likely be attributed to them thinking about the benefits as their own "earned right," an image that was purposefully intended by President Franklin D. Roosevelt at the program's inception. When his administration designed Social Security in 1934 and 1935, the president insisted on financing it entirely through payroll taxes, in order to cultivate the perception that benefits belong to those who have contributed to the system and thereby to secure for the program enduring political sustainability.[25] This strategy appears to have worked: indeed, the late Senator Daniel Patrick Moynihan famously called Social Security the "third rail of politics," and time and again it has survived efforts to scale it back. Yet this design likely renders many recipients likely to think of their future benefits simply as their own personal entitlement, not as part of a government-run system of social insurance. Similarly, in table 2.1, 39.8 percent of Medicare beneficiaries reported never having used a government program—a statistic reminiscent of the town meeting participant who told his congressman to "keep your government hands off my Medicare."[26]

As a caution, individuals' responses to the question about ever having used a "government social program" should not be regarded as the sole indicator of policy visibility, for various reasons. It was asked as the first question on a survey, before respondents had time to think about and remember their policy experiences. More importantly, among some Americans the term "government social program" likely evokes pejorative connotations of policies targeted to recipients they perceive as "undeserving." The case of the G.I. Bill, for which 40.3 percent answered in the negative, helps to shed light on beneficiaries' thinking in responding to this question. An in-depth study of World War II veteran beneficiaries found that despite the fact that the policy operated like a voucher program they could use at any college or vocational training school that admitted them, they regarded its source—government—to be quite unambiguous. Neither did this first generation of beneficiaries think of the G.I. Bill as an "earned right," but rather as the fruit of government's generosity. Yet they would not have considered it a "government social program" because its features did not conjure up the image that term evoked for them.[27]

These qualifications notwithstanding, what becomes apparent here is the paradox surrounding submerged features of American social policy: clearly, many citizens who might say they oppose government spending are in fact themselves beneficiaries of social programs. Among those who considered themselves supporters of the Tea Party movement in 2010, 18 percent reported that either they or a family member received Social Security benefits, compared to only 8 percent of non-supporters; for Medicare, the results were 16 and 9 percent, respectively. Yet these same individuals routinely voiced anti-government attitudes, with 92 percent of them saying they would prefer "a smaller government providing fewer services," compared to only 50 percent of the general public.[28] When a reporter asked sixty-two-year-old Tea Party activist Jodine White of Rocklin, California, how this could be, she answered, "That's a conundrum, isn't it? I don't know what to say. Maybe I don't want smaller government. I guess I want smaller government and my Social Security. I didn't look at it from the perspective of losing things I need."[29] Yet while Social Security possesses some features that may make recipients downplay its status as social provision, the policies that are fully immersed within the submerged state—channeled through tax expenditures and subsidies to private actors—are all the more likely to be completely overlooked by critics of government spending and by policy beneficiaries alike.

Shaping Views about Government

People are known to extrapolate from their own particular experiences of public policies in constructing their attitudes about government more generally. Political scientist Joe Soss discovered that beneficiaries of Social Security Disability Insurance (SSDI) encountered a responsive agency, one that actually answered their claims and complaints through routine bureaucratic procedures, albeit sometimes slow-moving ones. By contrast, beneficiaries of Aid to Families with Dependent Children (AFDC), the welfare program in place until 1996, found that agencies basically ignored them when they raised comparable issues. The AFDC beneficiaries were thus significantly less likely to believe that government was responsive to people like them, while the attitudes of the SSDI beneficiaries remained unaffected. Soss reasoned that the experience of policy receipt functioned for recipients like a microcosm of government generally: they drew lessons from it that they applied in constructing their broader attitudes about the political system. Thus, divergent policy experiences fostered disparate attitudes about government generally.[30] We have already seen that policies, depending on whether they are designed to be more visible or more submerged, vary in the level of awareness they generate among beneficiaries that government is their source. It stands to reason, then, that people's experiences of more submerged versus more visible policies might also influence their broader views about government.

The Governmental Issues Survey permits us to explore this possibility, comparing the influence of people's extent of usage of the more visible social programs versus those associated with the submerged state.[31] Respondents were asked whether they had ever used any of twelve direct social programs such as unemployment insurance, Pell Grants, Social Security, veterans' benefits, and several others. These can be classified as visible despite the fact that even they have some submerged characteristics, because they are visible relative to the policies of the submerged state. The average person reported having ever benefited from two such programs, and only one in five said they had never utilized any. The survey also allows us to consider usage of policies of the submerged state, in two ways. First, we can consider the number of particular tax expenditures individuals had ever utilized. When asked about each of four tax breaks—including the Home Mortgage Interest Deduction, 529 or Coverdell accounts, HOPE or Lifetime Learning Tax Credits, or the Child and Dependent Care Tax Credit—the average respondent reported having used one, while two in five respondents had not used any.[32] Second, we can gauge submerged state experiences by whether individuals possess tax-free employer-provided benefits. One in three respondents reported having a retirement savings plan through his or her employer, and one in two indicated having employer-sponsored health insurance. In fact, if we account for both usage of any of the four tax expenditures measured here and for the two types of employer-provided benefits, 74.9 percent of all respondents indicated that they have utilized at least one of these components of the submerged state—a figure not very different from the total that acknowledged having utilized at least one of the direct social programs, which was 79.5 percent. In short, usage of the policies of the submerged state is widespread and commonplace, rivaling that of the visible state.[33]

Now we can probe how individuals' usage of these different types of programs, some more visible and others belonging to the submerged state, related to their views of whether government is responsive to them. One question on the survey asked people for their level of agreement or disagreement with the statement "Government social programs have helped me in times of need." The answers to this question were widely distributed: 25 percent agreed strongly, 26 percent agreed somewhat, 7 percent neither agreed nor disagreed, 17 percent disagreed somewhat, and 25 percent disagreed strongly. Statistical analysis permits exploration of how social program usage may have influenced such views by comparing individuals who shared the same educational level, income, sex, race or ethnicity, and age, and differed only in the extent to which they experienced more visible policies or more submerged policies. This exercise revealed that *the larger the number of direct federal social programs an individual had ever used, the more likely he or she was to agree that government had helped in times of need.* All else equal, younger people and higher-income people were slightly less likely to agree than were other comparable individuals, but neither age nor income mattered nearly as much as did the total number of visible social programs individuals had ever used.[34] In separate analyses, I considered the effect of benefiting from policies of the submerged state, by testing for the number of tax expenditures individuals had ever used; whether they had a retirement savings plan through an employer; or if they possessed health insurance through their employer. *None of those more obscured policies, though they channel extensive resources to households and mean the loss of substantial government revenues, was significantly associated with beneficiaries' perception that government had helped them.*[35]

Respondents were also asked about their level of agreement with the statement "Government has given me opportunities to improve my standard of living." Once again, the responses were widely distributed, though they tilted in a more positive direction overall: 24 percent strongly agreed, 32 percent agreed somewhat, 2 percent neither agreed nor disagreed, 19 percent disagreed somewhat, and 23 percent strongly disagreed. Similar to the earlier results, comparing individuals with the same social and economic characteristics, *those who had utilized a greater number of the more visible policies were significantly more likely to feel that government had provided opportunities for them.* This time, all else equal, younger people were more likely to agree, as were more highly educated people, Hispanics, and men.[36] Conversely, turning to the submerged state policies, once again neither usage of tax-free employer-provided health insurance or retirement savings correlated to people's perception that government had improved their life chances. Interestingly, in one respect the submerged state yielded a significant relationship that diverged even more sharply from that of visible policies: *the greater the number of tax breaks an individual had benefited from, the more likely he or she was to disagree that government had provided opportunities for an improved standard of living.*[37] Despite the rhetoric surrounding policies such as the Home Mortgage Interest Deduction and higher education tax credits—that they provide opportunities for home-ownership and attending college—beneficiaries not only failed to attribute such effects to government, but moreover they actively disagreed that government generally had sought to improve their well-being.

The results suggest that the degree of visibility of the social programs Americans use may have a bearing on their attitudes about government more broadly: those who use more programs in which government's role is fairly obvious appear to acquire a heightened sense that government generally is responsive to them, whereas those who utilize policies of the submerged state do not. In fact, recipients of some hidden policies—namely, tax breaks—appear to be even less likely than other people to perceive that government has provided opportunities for them. This suggests that those who utilize policies of the submerged state—even if they find those provisions to be of value—do not recognize that it is government that benefits them.

Affecting Perceptions of Taxes

We might expect that tax breaks would at least be associated with more positive views about the tax system among recipients. This can also be explored using the Governmental Issues Survey. One question asked respondents whether they felt that the amount they were asked to pay in federal income taxes was "more than [their] fair share," their "fair share," or "less than [their] fair share." In answering, 56 percent reported that they were asked to pay their "fair share," whereas 40 percent said they paid "more than their fair share."[38] Given that tax expenditures reduce claimants' tax burdens, it would seem reasonable to expect that individuals who utilize a greater number of such benefits might gain a more positive outlook on the fairness of federal income taxes than those who utilize fewer, all else equal. The evidence for this is lacking: the sum of such policies individuals have ever used, of the four mentioned earlier, yielded no significant effect on their attitudes about tax fairness. Factors strongly associated with this view instead include, among other factors, education (those who have more education are more likely to feel they pay less than their fair share) and income (those who have more income are more likely to feel that they pay more than their fair share), but usage of tax breaks did not register an impact.[39] Likewise, neither did usage of either employer-provided health insurance or retirement savings seem to mitigate recipients' views of tax fairness, regardless of the enormous drain these benefits impose on federal budgets.[40] Paradoxically, tax expenditures, although they permit Americans to pay significantly less in taxes, do not correspond with more sanguine views about the tax system.

By contrast, moreover, using visible government social programs does seem to foster salutary views about tax fairness: comparing individuals with similar socioeconomic circumstances and demographic characteristics, those who have used more of these policies are significantly more likely to feel that they paid "less than [their] fair share" in taxes.[41] Individuals' sense of having benefited from government through visible social programs appears to mitigate their sense of being burdened by it through taxes, while usage of policies embedded in the submerged state does not.

Shaping Political Action

Finally, we consider how beneficiaries of direct versus submerged social policies compare in terms of the extent to which they undertake political action that is motivated by their concerns about the policies they utilize. We have already seen at the beginning of this chapter that the submerged state cultivates active engagement among the interest groups that benefit from it; now we investigate the extent to which it engenders advocacy among the people who use its benefits. In the survey, all respondents were asked whether they had ever participated in voting or in making campaign contributions. Later on, after they indicated which social policies they had utilized, beneficiaries of each policy who had previously reported that they had ever voted were asked if they had ever "taken into account the position of a candidate on the [program used] in deciding either how to vote or whether to vote." Likewise, beneficiaries who said that they had ever made campaign contributions were asked whether they did so, "at least in part, because of your concern about [program used]." The

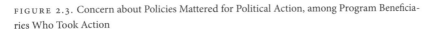

FIGURE 2.3. Concern about Policies Mattered for Political Action, among Program Beneficiaries Who Took Action

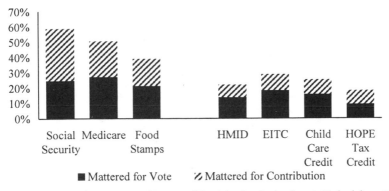

■ Mattered for Vote   ⊘ Mattered for Contribution

Source: Social and Governmental Issues and Participation Study of 2008. Methodology: U.S. national survey conducted by Survey Research Institute at Cornell University, August 23, 2008– November 1, 2008, N = 1,400.

percent answering in the affirmative to each question is indicated, respectively, by the solid and striped sections of the bars in figure 2.3.

This figure makes apparent that among Americans who have ever utilized submerged policies, those policy experiences barely factor into their motivation for political action, doing so considerably less than their experiences of more visible social policies. Rates of policy-focused political action among beneficiaries of more visible policies, clustered on the left, are markedly higher than among beneficiaries of submerged policies, clustered on the right. That beneficiaries of Social Security and Medicare targeted their efforts toward the policies that help them is not surprising, given that they are known to be mobilized by political parties and groups such as the American Association of Retired Persons (AARP) to do so.[42] But beneficiaries of food stamps are not regularly mobilized by groups or officials, and yet they are much more likely to have taken political action focused on that policy than were beneficiaries of any of the tax breaks toward their policies. Among food stamps beneficiaries, 21 percent reported that they had ever taken into account the position of a candidate on that issue in deciding how to vote, compared to only 14 percent of Home Mortgage Interest Deduction beneficiaries; among food stamp beneficiaries who had made campaign contributions, 17.7 percent had done so in part because of their concerns about that program, compared to only 8.1 percent of HMID users. Policy visibility appears to act independently of socioeconomic characteristics of beneficiaries; among the tax policy beneficiaries, in fact, the highest rates of policy-focused activity occurred among recipients of EITC, the policy geared toward low-income people, which happens to be delivered in a manner that makes it somewhat more visible than the others.

These disparities in policy-focused action flow logically from the differences in the visibility of policies: if beneficiaries barely associate their provisions with government, it stands to reason that usage is unlikely to motivate their political action. Such disparities may have ripple effects on political mobilization rates: it can hardly be worth the time of groups and officials to attempt to activate people to advocate for a particular policy if they do not even think of it as emanating from government. In short, whereas the submerged state energizes the interest groups that benefit from its existence, its policies do little to engender political mobilization among ordinary Americans—for example, to press for more equitable benefits.

Degenerative Politics

The submerged state generates politics that are not only undemocratic but, worse, have degenerative effects on the relationship between citizens and government.[43] Its policies easily capture and hold the attention of organized interests, which are quick to mobilize for the preservation of the status quo. Simultaneously, however, the same policies fail to make themselves apparent as social programs to most citizens who use them, and they do not appear to convey to beneficiaries any broader messages about either government's responsiveness to them or the fairness of the tax system. Beneficiaries of some tax breaks are, perversely, more convinced than other citizens that government has failed to provide them with opportunities—although some of the policies they utilize aim to do just that. Policies of the submerged state thus stand in contrast to more visible policies, the usage of which is associated with citizens' understanding that government helps them in times of needs and provides opportunities to them, and that the tax system is fair.

These divergent political effects of the submerged state have several implications for American politics. First, efforts to reform such policies, as undertaken by the Obama administration, face uphill battles. Opponents will likely meet reformers quickly, armed and ready for battle, poised to defend the policies that have benefited them so abundantly. By contrast, ordinary citizens are unlikely to realize what is at stake in the efforts or to offer assistance. Rather, they will act complacently and remain uninformed. Reform efforts, therefore, even if they are motivated to address the needs of ordinary citizens, quickly devolve into elite battles, engaging political leaders and interest groups but not Americans generally. Transformation of the submerged state is thus a high-risk endeavor—one that poses many immediate obstacles to proponents, and that may yield the unintended effect of further alienating from the political process the very people it intends to assist. These patterns became pronounced in 2009–10, as we will see in chapters 4 and 5.

Second, the political rewards of reform—at least in the near term—may be very few. Even if reformers succeed in terminating or refashioning policies of the submerged state to respond more effectively to the needs of most citizens, they are unlikely to reap the benefits of such efforts come Election Day. Certainly interest groups will continue to fill the campaign coffers especially of their devout supporters, but the electorate is unlikely to recognize the meaning and value of what has been accomplished. Citizens may, furthermore, be so aggravated by the empowerment of groups that they become more disaffected politically and less inclined to participate themselves.

Third, to the extent that political officials choose to expand further the submerged state, this strategy will be counterproductive to efforts to renew the relationship between government and citizens. This will be the case even if reformers strive to make policies such as tax expenditures more accessible to those who are less well-off: as we have seen, such policies do not foster salutary attitudes toward government or civic engagement. In fact, they may, to the contrary, make citizens more resentful of government.

Reconstituting the submerged state successfully requires that reformers pay apt attention to conveying what is at stake to the public, through political communication, policy design, and the manner of program delivery. We will now turn to examine how this could be done.

3 · FROM *NUDGE* TO REVEAL

WITH MATT GUARDINO

In October 2010, at a barbecue hosted by a Republican women's club in Huntersville, North Carolina, a reporter asked guests what had happened to their taxes since Barack Obama had become president. Replied Bob Paratore, age fifty-nine, "Federal and state have both gone up." Others agreed. The reporter reminded the group that the stimulus bill in early 2009 had cut taxes for 95 percent of working Americans. Paratore conceded, "You're right, you're right. I'll be honest with you: it was so subtle that personally, I didn't notice it." He was not alone: a poll conducted just a month previous found that only about one out of ten Americans were aware that the Obama administration had lowered taxes for most Americans, and one-quarter of those polled believed taxes had been increased.[1]

In fact, the invisibility of the new Making Work Pay tax cut was perfectly in keeping with the characteristics of the submerged state: people benefited from it without even knowing it. In fact, some even believed they had been penalized rather than having benefited. What was especially remarkable, though, was that in this instance, the "subtlety" was no unintended consequence. Rather, advisers in the Obama administration had deliberately planned for the tax breaks to be hidden.

They followed the advice of behavioral economists who have found that how people *perceive* an infusion of money influences whether they spend or save it. These experts argue that past tax cuts failed to stimulate the economy because when people receive money in a lump sum, it tends not to affect their consumption habits. Therefore, in order to encourage Americans to spend, policymakers purposefully set up the Making Work Pay tax breaks in the stimulus so that individuals would have less tax withholding taken out of each paycheck throughout the year, thus bringing home slightly larger amounts in each pay period.[2] In effect, officials designed these benefits—already hidden by being placed in the tax system rather than distributed as relief payments—to be even more highly obscured than if they had been delivered as tax rebates.

What the behavioral economists overlooked, however, is how those arrangements would affect citizens' view of the political system. Unaware of the new benefits and whom they assisted, Americans became increasingly convinced that the Obama administration was not responsive to people like them. One state representative who attended the North Carolina barbecue summed it up aptly, "This was the tax cut that fell in the woods—nobody heard it."[3] While many had heard of the price tag for the stimulus—$787 billion—they were unaware that one out of three of those dollars lowered the taxes of most Americans. Thus, a policy that should have given Americans a sense that government was making a difference in their lives failed completely to do so. Obama himself acknowledged later on that the policy's invisible delivery "was the right thing to do economically, but politically it meant that nobody knew that they were getting a tax cut. . . . And in fact what ended up happening was six months into it, or nine months into it, people had thought we had raised their taxes instead of cutting their taxes."[4]

Yet the "submerged state" need not remain hidden from ordinary Americans and be visible only to entrenched powerful interests. In order to understand how to "reveal" its policies and how they function, it is appropriate to follow the lead of behavioral economists insofar as they use evidence-based social science, particularly experiments, to understand how policies influence people's responses. However, instead of focusing only on the social and economic effects of policies, we need to turn the spotlight to their political effects. We should examine how policies themselves influence citizens' awareness of their existence, of who benefits from them, and of government's role in providing them. These effects are basic to understanding how policies shape citizens' attitudes about government and their engagement in politics. To facilitate these goals, this chapter considers the results of an experiment that explored how providing citizens with basic information about submerged policies would influence their likelihood of forming opinions about them and their levels of support for them. This experiment and others point to how policymakers can through policy design, policy delivery, and political communication—pull back the camouflage that obscures the submerged state and alert citizens to its effects.

The Value of Evidence-Based Social Science: From Economics to Political Science

Behavioral economists, drawing on observations from psychology, criticize the standard economic model of human behavior for exaggerating the extent of human beings' rationality, willpower, and selfishness. Through their research, they find that when most of us make actual choices in real life, we often deviate from economists' usual assumptions: for example, our default is to be bound by inertia, and therefore we are prone to procrastination; we tend to focus on the present, and as a result do a poor job of planning for the future. Thus, many people would like to lose weight by next week, but they don't manage to get themselves to exercise or to eat healthier food today; they want to save for retirement some years from now, but fail to take measures presently to do so. Researchers also find that people are easily influenced not merely by the real value of choices but also by how they are framed and presented.[5]

On a less gloomy note, however, behavioral economists reason that people's natural inertia can be effectively harnessed through mechanisms that prompt them to make "good" choices, the ones they would prefer themselves to make. Richard Thaler and Cass Sunstein refer to such arrangements as "choice architecture," means by which to "nudge" people through "libertarian paternalism" to behave in ways that promote more efficient outcomes. Public policies can serve as such tools if they are designed and delivered in ways that provide incentives that facilitate good decision-making.[6] For example, if people have to take the initiative to sign themselves up for a tax-deductible, tax-deferred 401(k) retirement plan, even one to which their employer would contribute on their behalf, many will fail to do so.[7] If the program is set up to enroll them automatically unless they opt out, however, the vast majority will participate: one study of women only found that just 36 percent took the initiative to join such plans, but 86 percent remained in once enrollment was conducted on their behalf.[8]

As indicated by this example, behavioral economics can offer useful insights to policymakers about how people respond to the details of policy design and delivery. As Sendhil Mullainathan explains, "The difference in impact between two broad policies may not be as great as the difference in how each policy is framed—its deadlines, implementation, and the design of its physical appearance . . . the devil really is in the details."[9] While much of the debate over policies revolves around broad values such as the appropriate role of government versus markets, the success of policies may depend less on the ideals of their framers than on the specific instruments and processes through which citizens become aware of policy availability and apply for or claim benefits.

Anyone who has ever attempted to complete a Free Application for Federal Student Aid (FAFSA) form—which functions as the gateway to student loans, Pell Grants, and other forms of federal financial aid—is well familiar with the extensive amount of time and attention to detail it requires. Scholars have long suspected that the complexity of the financial aid application process likely acts as a deterrent to college enrollment among less advantaged young people. A group of economists devised an experiment in which H&R Block tax professionals assisted randomly selected high school seniors from low- to moderate-income families in completing the FAFSA, offered them an estimate of the amount of aid for which they would be eligible, and gave them information about local colleges. Students from that group were significantly more likely to enroll in college and to receive aid than either those in the control group, who received no assistance or information, or those in a second treatment group, which received only information.[10] Such findings have prompted policymakers to seek means to simplify the FAFSA, enabling much of it to be filled in automatically with information from tax forms.

As indicated by this example, insights from behavioral economics derive their credibility from rigorous research, typically conducted in the form of experiments. Most studies in the social sciences, regardless of how carefully constructed they are, leave analysts with uncertainties about causal effects. The possibility often lingers that the evidence used is biased in some way that may lead to faulty conclusions. For example, say that we want to study the effects of usage of a particular public policy, and plan to use survey data collected at a single point in time to do so. The problem is that if policy recipients differed from non-recipients in some preexisting characteristic possessed before program usage, and that feature in turn influences the subsequent behavior in which we are interested, we might inaccurately assume that their experience of the policy caused the outcome when in fact it was only incidental. Of course, scholars do their best to control for as many relevant factors as possible, but we do not always know what all of those may be, nor do we necessarily have the means of controlling for each one of them.

The value of experiments is that they permit us to assign people *randomly* to particular treatment groups, so that each individual is as likely as any other to take part in any treatment group or in the control group. This process, usually conducted through a computer-generated random number series, alleviates the possibility of such bias.[11] As with the randomized trials used to test the effectiveness of new drugs, such procedures allow us to isolate causal effects with greater confidence than do non-experimental approaches. Certainly experiments leave their own lingering questions, namely, whether the same results would be generated in the "real world," outside of experimental conditions. These can be reduced, however, through repeated trials, using experimental designs that test multiple variations of phenomena, and with field experiments that model actual circumstances. Such evidence-based research makes the findings highly valuable to policymakers.

The chief limitation of the behavioral economics approach, however, is that it largely ignores the fundamental purpose of American government as most citizens understand it: to be "government of the people, by the people, for the people," or, in short, to be democratic. Behavioral economists are generally concerned about whether "choice architecture" prompts desirable social and economic outcomes—such as more high school graduates, more retirement savings, fewer overweight people, and less consumption of energy resources. Proponents assume that such outcomes are "better" because they are more efficient—for example, by leading to a more highly skilled workforce, less economic insecurity, better health and lower health care spending, and less waste. While those goals are laudable, pursuing them does not necessarily foster democratic citizenship, for example, by enhancing citizens' ability to be aware of government actions, to form opinions about them, and to be able to take a stand on them. In fact, the pursuit of some policy goals—depending on how it is conducted and the design of the policies created—may inadvertently prove detrimental to citizens' knowledge and agency, as indicated by the example of the stimulus tax breaks discussed earlier.

Political scientists have also engaged in experimental research over the past two decades, and many of their studies do shed light on how to enhance the practice of democracy. The most substantial accumulation of knowledge pertains to the effectiveness of various "get out the vote" strategies, which have been tested through field experiments. These studies, spearheaded by Donald Green and Alan Gerber of Yale University and their collaborators, demonstrate that impersonal approaches such as direct mail and robotic calls do little to elevate voter turnout. By contrast, they find that more personal approaches, such as door-to-door canvassing and calls from volunteers, can be quite effective, boosting turnout among groups that are typically less engaged, such as the young, low-income people, and minorities.[12] Other valuable experimental studies illuminate such topics as the impact of elite messages or media coverage on political attitudes. Diana Mutz, for example, utilizes a laboratory experiment to demonstrate that exposure to a range of political views fosters tolerance: "If people are surrounded by people who think much like they do, they will be less aware of the legitimate arguments on the other side of contemporary political controversies."[13]

Yet while these and other experimental studies by political scientists do shed light on how some aspects of politics influence the health of democracy, unlike the work of behavioral economists, they rarely focus on the instruments of governance—public policies.[14] As a result, we know little about how the design and delivery of public policies shape outcomes such as citizens' awareness and understanding of them, their support for them, or their likelihood of taking action.

Experimental approaches could be especially useful for studying how the submerged state and the politics surrounding it affect citizens' views about it. Precisely because policies such as tax expenditures are so "hidden" by their design, questions about them on standard surveys are unlikely to yield reliable measures: we cannot expect people to express meaningful views about something they know little or nothing about. Complicating matters further, citizens' level of information about tax policy generally is biased by their own socioeconomic characteristics. A 2003 poll conducted by the Kaiser Family Foundation found that knowledge of the tax code is highly correlated with income: a majority of the richest 5 percent answered questions about tax policy correctly, whereas only about 20 percent of the remainder of the population did.[15] This information bias begs the question of how the views of citizens—especially those who are not affluent—might be affected if they were better informed about these policies. The experimental method can allow us to alter precisely the amount and type of information individuals possess about these policies and to test the influence of such variation.

Designing an Experiment in Revealing the Submerged State

A central question emerging from the inquiry in this book thus far is what difference would it make if the submerged state were revealed to citizens? In other words, what if citizens were informed about the existence of its specific policies and their redistributive effects? Would they become more engaged, at least by registering opinions about such policies? And would they lend them their support or not?

Scholars of public opinion have not previously investigated this specific question. In the past, decades of survey research showed abysmally low levels of general political knowledge on the part of many citizens, casting doubt on their ability or interest to process political information in a meaningful way.[16] Contemporary scholars might also point out that public policies are usually the subject of partisan and ideologically framed debate dominated by political elites: people rarely receive straight, unidimensional information.[17] And political scientists have found that sometimes new information simply reinforces people's misperceptions, especially if they are political partisans who already have strong views about particular subjects.[18]

These concerns about the limitations of the value of political information should not, however, deter us from considering whether revealing the submerged state could help citizens to formulate views about it. Particular characteristics of submerged policies may heighten the potential value of information about it. First, policies of the submerged state have not been the subject of sustained and extensive partisan elite debate, certainly not the kind of debate that is sufficiently loud and widespread to reach the vast majority of citizens. Rather, they have been enacted and maintained in the realm of what political scientist Jacob Hacker terms "subterranean" politics, rather than in highly visible partisan trench warfare.[19] Second, the lack of much overt controversy over such policies discourages coverage by the news media, which largely follows elite cues and is drawn to dramatic conflict. For both of these reasons, people are less likely to have rigidly formulated views on policies of the submerged state, and thus new information is more likely to make a meaningful difference in their opinion articulation.

Recently, moreover, scholars have developed a more nuanced understanding of when and how citizens do process political information effectively. Generally speaking, those who understand and pay attention to the political system are better able to process policy-relevant messages in ways that are meaningful, in the sense that they are consistent with their own underlying political and social predispositions.[20] Also, if citizens possess in-depth information about some particular aspect of politics, it can supplement their general political knowledge and facilitate their ability to form opinions.[21] For example, women and African Americans are more likely than other citizens to be informed about gender and race issues, respectively.[22] Martin Gilens has actually examined how views about public policies are influenced by new political information. He finds that the provision of policy-related facts does influence opinion formation, in ways that are contingent on individuals' general political knowledge. The information conveyed to respondents in his study, however, pertained not to the details of policies themselves but rather to contextual information, such as crime rates or the size of the deficit.[23] The impact of actual details about how policies work and their basic effects had yet to be tested, and my collaborator, Matt Guardino, and I set out to do just that.

Extrapolating from what scholars already know, we expected that specific information about public policies—presented in a straightforward, concise, yet accurate manner—could assist citizens in forming opinions about them. In addition, we anticipated that such information could enable them to adopt views that reflected their underlying interests and values. To explore these expectations, we designed a randomized general population experiment to test how the provision of information about tax expenditures influences individuals' opinions about them. The experiment was administered via the Internet on a survey of a nationally representative general population sample.[24]

We set up the experiment to examine how exposure to different types and degrees of information influence opinion formation and support, comparing subjects who received (1) no information (the control condition); (2) a basic description of policy goals and mechanisms, similar to what policymakers occasionally convey but without a partisan slant or rhetorical style; and (3) the basic description plus information on the distribution of policy benefits by income group, details that are rarely ever provided about such policies. We aimed to explore the impact of such variation both between groups of people subjected to different treatments (a "between-subjects" design) and within groups who experienced more than one treatment condition ("within-subjects").[25] We divided a national sample of 526 adults into three randomly selected groups. Within each group, we investigated levels of support for three major tax expenditures: two that primarily benefit upper-income people, the Home Mortgage Interest Tax Deduction (HMID) and the Retirement Savings Contribution Tax Credit, and one that primarily benefits lower-income individuals, the Earned Income Tax Credit (EITC).

The *basic information treatment*, applied to Group 1, was designed to assess the extent to which the provision of a neutral description of the basic purposes and mechanisms of tax expenditure policies might spur opinion expression and change. At the start, subjects were asked their opinions on each of the three tax expenditures without being provided with prior information about the policies. For example, subjects were asked: "Do you favor or oppose the Home Mortgage Interest Tax Deduction?" Possible responses included "favor strongly," "favor somewhat," "oppose somewhat," "oppose strongly," and "don't know/no opinion."[26] Their answer at this stage represents the control condition. Next, we distracted these same subjects with a series of three apolitical questions about sports and entertainment. After this, they were provided with two-sentence descriptions of each policy, as follows:

> Now, here is some information about the federal Home Mortgage Interest Tax Deduction. This policy is a tax benefit for homeowners. It allows them to reduce the amount they pay in income taxes based on the amount they pay in interest on their home mortgage.

Then subjects were once again asked for their opinions, with the same question wording as above, yielding responses to the basic information treatment.

The *full information treatment* exposed subjects to the same basic description as Group 1, plus concise information about the relative financial benefits that flow to various income groups as a result of the policies. As in the basic information treatment, subjects were first asked for their opinions about the policies without being offered information about them. Then, after the same series of distraction questions asked of Group 1, they were given the same description as that group, but it was supplemented by two sentences about which income groups gain the most and by a graph depicting the distribution of benefits (fig. 3.1), as follows:

> The people who benefit most from this policy are those who have the highest incomes. In 2005, a large majority of the benefits went to people who lived in households that made $100,000 or more that year.

Next, subjects were again asked for their opinions of each policy.

We also asked all subjects a series of questions about their partisan and ideological orientation, level of general political knowledge, concern about rising economic inequality, and experiences with tax policy, as well as basic demographic information.[27]

Informing Citizens

The experiment's basic results indicate, as anticipated, that policy information does indeed enable people to form opinions. Those who had previously been reticent to answer when asked their view of specific tax expenditures, once given information about them became willing to take a stand. Table 3.1 shows the distributions of opinion following each information

FIGURE 3.1. Who Benefits from the Home Mortgage Interest Deduction?

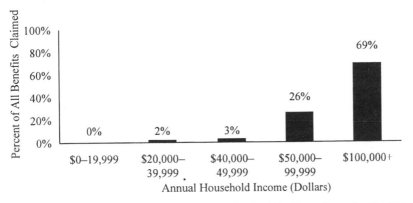

Source. Joint Committee on Taxation, "Estimates of Federal Tax Expenditures for Fiscal Years 2006 2010" (April 25, 2006), http://www.jct.gov/publications.html?func=startdown&id=1199.

TABLE 3.1. Effects of Information Treatments on Views about Tax Expenditures (%)

	Home Mortgage Interest Deduction			Retirement Savings Contribution Tax Credit			Earned Income Tax Credit		
	Favor	Oppose	Don't Know	Favor	Oppose	Don't Know	Favor	Oppose	Don't Know
Basic Information (*N* = 171)									
Pre-	64.5	6.9	28.6	56.8	7.5	35.7	58.2	11.7	30.8
Post-	80.7	5.5	13.9	74.9	11.6	13.4	70.4	20.7	8.8
Difference	+16.2	−1.4	−14.7	+18.1	+4.1	−22.3	+12.2	+9.0	−22.0
Full Information (*N* = 177)									
Pre-	54.8	7.1	35.7	53.0	5.3	41.7	52.6	15.1	32.4
Post-	39.7	40.8	19.5	48.8	35.3	15.9	75.3	15.8	9.0
Difference	−15.1	+33.7	−16.2	−4.2	+30.0	−25.8	+22.7	+0.7	−23.4

Source: Time-Sharing Experiments for the Social Sciences 2008, Mettler-Guardino Study.

treatment and the difference between them.[28] In each of the six experiments, the provision of information about the policy allowed many people who had previously answered only "don't know" to register a viewpoint either in support or opposition.[29] The percentage of respondents offering no opinion was at least cut in half in each case, and it dropped more precipitously in some: after gaining more information about EITC, for example, the percentage answering "don't know" declined from nearly one in three respondents to fewer than one in ten.

In addition, the results show that the provision of information prompted people to develop different positions depending on the type and amount of the information conveyed. The basic information treatment fostered, on net, greater support for all three policies.[30] For example, for the Home Mortgage Interest Deduction (HMID), the proportion of subjects expressing a favorable attitude increased from 64.5 percent to 80.7 percent, and the ranks of the opposed declined just slightly, from 6.9 percent to 5.5 percent; the response for the Retirement Savings Contribution Tax Credit was similar. These reactions are not surprising, given that generalized social images of "target groups" are known to influence citizens' levels of favorability toward a number of U.S. domestic policies.[31] The shifts in support for the HMID comport with the generally positive image enjoyed by this policy as one that facilitates the ideal of private home-ownership—a powerful image in U.S. culture, one that is central to the American dream of upward socioeconomic mobility. In addition, the eligible group would likely appear to be most citizens, given that as of 2000 fully 66.2 percent of Americans owned homes.[32] Similarly, workers saving for retirement are also thought of as a worthy group, deserving of public support, and as a group that could include most Americans. Thus, it makes sense that when subjects were informed in basic language about what these two policies entail, they became more favorable toward them. These results suggest that when people are informed only about the basic functions of the policies—the typical information policymakers usually convey, if they speak of them at all—support for them grows.

The second treatment, however, in which people became informed of the actual distributive effects of tax expenditures, produced dramatically different results.[33] In the case of the two policies that disproportionately benefit the affluent, once respondents realized that fact, support for each declined and opposition grew dramatically—by 33.7 and 30.0 percentage points, respectively. Information about their upwardly distributive implications trumped the policy's positive images—in other words, specific policy facts became more salient as the basis for opinion expression than widely held social and cultural representations. It should be noted that in the case of neither policy did opposition grow sufficiently to overwhelm support, though the two positions reached parity in the case of the HMID. Nonetheless, the scope of the change in people's opinions, after receiving only a small bit of policy information, is striking; possibly more extensive and sustained information could promote more extensive transformation of existing views.

In the case of the EITC, once people realized that it actually helps low-income people, support grew by a full 22.7 percentage points. In fact, while opposition had grown by 9.0 percentage points in response to the basic treatment, the distributive information curtailed that effect: opposition barely changed at all from the pre-treatment or "control" position. Overall, this downwardly distributive policy enjoyed much more widespread endorsement among full information respondents (75.3 percent) than did either of the other two policies (39.7 and 48.8 percent, respectively).[34]

These effects of the distributive treatment are quite striking, suggesting that if Americans were more informed of who actually benefits from government policies, that opposition to those favoring the affluent would grow and support for those aiding the less well-off would increase, too. We will discuss this in greater depth shortly, but first we will explore how new information facilitated opinion formation and for whom.

Broadening the Ranks of Who Takes a Stand

Some people routinely pay attention to politics and seek to be well-informed about political issues and how government works, and others do not. Knowing about such matters constitutes a basic form of political engagement. Political scientists have learned that the patterns determining which Americans know more about politics is not randomly distributed. Michael X. Delli Carpini and Scott Keeter report that when Americans are asked basic questions about politics, men answer correctly 1.35 times more often than women; pre–baby boomers, 1.38 times more than post–baby boomers; affluent people, 1.59 times more than poor people; and whites, twice as often as blacks.[35] In short, rates of political knowledge are organized by sex, age, class, and race. Despite the fact that the formal structures that mandated some of these forms of inequality in the past have long since been dismantled, nonetheless informal social and political practices still perpetuate such disparities.

Matt Guardino and I wanted to understand how providing individuals with information about public policies influences the composition of the ranks of those who register an opinion about them. Given what is known about political knowledge, we'd expect that in the absence of efforts to inform the public—in the parlance of experiments, in the "control" condition—the people who are most likely to have opinions about policies will be those who are affluent, older, white, and male; conversely, those who are poor, younger, black, and female will be much less likely to hold views. The question is, what difference is made by the provision of new policy-specific information: does it merely exacerbate the opinion-generating advantage of people who are already highly knowledgeable, or does it "democratize" the ranks of those willing to take a stand on an issue? Existing research would lead to a prediction that new information may very well exacerbate the inequality between opinionated and quiescent citizens. This is because scholars have found that those who possess more general knowledge about politics are usually best poised to incorporate new information that they receive, as they have the capacity to put it in the context of their already substantial knowledge base and are thus able to make sense of it and to form an opinion about it.[36]

In order to assess this, we needed to test respondents' general political knowledge. We did so by administering to all subjects a standard five-item battery of questions, which asked such things as which party currently holds the majority in the U.S. House of Representatives, and whose responsibility it is to determine if a law is constitutional or not.[37] We then divided the sample into three segments that we identified as possessing high, moderate, and low levels of such knowledge, and analyzed patterns of opinion-taking accordingly.[38]

Table 3.2 examines the rates of opinion formation—of those changing their answer from "don't know/no opinion" prior to receiving policy information to registering an opinion afterward—for people with low, moderate, and high levels of general political knowledge. As we would expect, prior to new information, "don't know/no opinion" responses were by far the least common among individuals with the highest rates of general

TABLE 3.2. Rates of Opinion Formation as Indicated by "Don't Know" Responses Before and After Information Treatment, by Level of General Political Knowledge (%)

	Home Mortgage Interest Deduction			Retirement Savings Contribution Tax Credit			Earned Income Tax Credit		
	\multicolumn{9}{c}{Level of General Political Knowledge}								
	Low	Moderate	High	Low	Moderate	High	Low	Moderate	High
Basic Information (N = 171)									
Pre-	35.3	48.0	15.1	41.2	47.1	26.4	22.9	27.5	34.5
Post-	17.1	19.6	9.4	29.4	17.6	4.7	9.1	7.8	10.6
Difference	−18.2	−28.4	−5.7	−11.8	−29.5	−21.7	−13.8	−19.7	−23.9
Full Information (N = 177)									
Pre-	60.0	37.5	29.5	44.7	50.0	36.9	30.3	26.2	36.2
Post-	40.0	11.9	13.8	35.0	9.3	10.6	20.5	7.0	5.3
Difference	−20.0	−25.6	−15.7	−9.7	−40.7	−26.2	−9.8	−19.2	−30.9

Source: Time-Sharing Experiments for the Social Sciences 2008, Mettler-Guardino Study.

political knowledge. The provision of new information lessened the typical disparities in opinion expression. It proved to facilitate opinion-taking quite widely, prompting subjects in all general knowledge categories to exhibit an increased propensity to articulate policy opinions.[39]

In the case of the upwardly distributive policies, subjects with moderate levels of political knowledge proved at least as or more likely than the others to respond and to take a stand once provided with policy-specific details. These results revealed a curvilinear dynamic: those with moderate levels of general political knowledge exhibited the strongest propensity to use specific facts about tax expenditures to help them express preferences. In response to the basic information treatment, the percentage of this group choosing the "don't know" response declined by 28.4 percentage points in the case of the Home Mortgage Interest Deduction, and by 29.5 percentage points in the case of the Retirement Savings Contribution Tax Credit; in response to the full information treatment, these rates declined by 25.6 and 40.7 percentage points, respectively. In each case, smaller percentages of low- and high-knowledge individuals shifted toward opinion expression, although the changes were still quite dramatic.[40]

Thus, the provision of information helped equalize the rate of opinion formation between middle- and high-knowledge subjects, and brought the frequency of opinion expression among low-knowledge subjects closer to that of more knowledgeable subjects, even though it still lagged behind. This pattern makes sense given that both low- and high-knowledge people are known to possess distinct characteristics that can inhibit information effects in some cases. Those with low levels of general political knowledge may lack either the cognitive capacity or the contextual information to facilitate comprehension and use of specific facts to express policy preferences. Those with high levels of knowledge may be less influenced by new information because even prior to receiving it, their stronger political reasoning capacities and more intense and ideologically coherent value predispositions already led them to express opinions, and because those same factors may make them reluctant to be swayed by a mere new factoid.[41]

In analyzing the impact of new information on opinions regarding the EITC, however, we found a different dynamic at work. Here, general political knowledge appeared to be strongly and positively related to opinion expression. While specific information on the EITC spurred attitude expression in all knowledge groups, the magnitude of the shift increased substantially from low- to moderate- to high-knowledge subjects. The basic information treatment fostered a rise in opinion articulation of 13.8 percentage points among the low-knowledge subjects, 19.7 percentage points among moderate-knowledge subjects, and 23.9 percentage points among the high-knowledge subjects; the full information treatment sparked increases of 9.8, 19.2, and 30.9 percentage points, respectively.

Notably, those with high levels of general political knowledge had started out *less* likely to offer opinions about the EITC than those with less political knowledge. This finding prompted us to consider actual reported usage rates of these policies, which we had asked about near the end of our questionnaire.[42] Usage of the upwardly distributive policies appears to be directly related to levels of general political knowledge: 40.7 percent of those with a high level of knowledge had used the Home Mortgage Interest Deduction, compared to 24 percent of those with a low level of political knowledge; for the Retirement Savings Contribution Tax Credit, these rates were 32 and 13.5 percent, respectively. Yet the reverse pattern occurred in the case of the EITC: fully 39.4 percent of those with low general knowledge rates have used it, compared to just 13.6 percent of those with high-knowledge rates. This relationship is not surprising, given that the EITC is targeted specifically at low-income citizens, and rates of political knowledge tend to be correlated with socioeconomic factors.[43] Therefore, in the case of the EITC, a large percentage of subjects with low levels of general political knowledge already knew something about this policy—because they experienced its benefits directly—whereas those who are typically well-informed about politics were especially likely to find themselves unable to register an opinion at the outset. However, these subjects with higher levels of general knowledge readily increased their rates of opinion articulation once they became more informed about the EITC.

In sum, our results suggest that receiving policy-specific information can spur greater opinion expression among citizens, even on issues that are often regarded as complex and arcane. On upwardly distributive policies, new information permitted those with moderate levels of preexisting general political knowledge to increase their rates of opinion formation most significantly; other groups also became more willing to articulate their views, though the differences were not as substantial. Notably, in such cases the provision of policy-specific information had a democratizing effect, spurring the most basic form of political engagement—opinion formation—even among many who typically refrain from taking a stand.

Voicing Opinions That Make Sense

Now we investigate whether providing citizens with information about tax expenditures helps them to voice opinions that "make sense," in that they reflect their own material interests and their ideological and partisan inclinations. First, focusing on the full information treatment, we examined how individuals' responses were influenced by their income levels.[44]

Figure 3.2 presents the results of the full information treatments on opinions about the Home Mortgage Interest Deduction by respondents' income level.[45] As we expected, low- and middle-income subjects, once informed that this policy mostly benefits the affluent, shifted their opinions significantly from overwhelming support to opposition. The scope of the change was especially dramatic among low-income citizens, whose level of support plummeted from 49.1 percent pre-treatment to 17 percent post-treatment, while their opposition surged from 6.8 to 57.6 percent. Results among middle-income subjects were similar but somewhat less pronounced: support dropped from 53.6 to 38.2 percent, while opposition jumped from 10.1 to 45.6 percent.[46] Among high-income respondents, support for the HMID increased after being offered information about its distributive effects, though only modestly, from 62 percent pre-treatment to 69.3 percent, but, contrary to what we anticipated, their opposition to the policy also grew moderately—from 4 to 14.3 percent. Overall, these results strongly suggest that specific information about distributive effects of this policy did indeed help citizens to align their opinions with their material interests.

The same experiment produced very similar results in the case of the Retirement Savings Contribution Tax Credit, as seen in figure 3.3. Favorable opinions among low-income subjects dropped from 50 percent

FIGURE 3.2. Effects of Full Information on Views of Home Mortgage Interest Deduction, by Income Group (%)

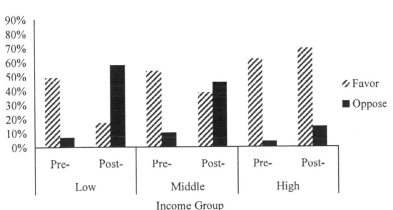

Source: Time-Sharing Experiments for the Social Sciences 2008, Mettler-Guardino Study.

pre-treatment to 23.6 percent post-treatment, while opposition surged from 3.4 to 52.5 percent. Among middle-income citizens, favorability decreased slightly, from 51.5 to 47.1 percent, but opposition increased more than fourfold, from 8.9 to 41.1 percent. Among affluent subjects, becoming informed that this tax credit especially benefits those in their income group sparked an increase in support from 60 to 80 percent. Interestingly, however, just as in the case of the HMID, information also sparked a mild increase in opposition among this group, from 2 to 8 percent.[47] Once again, information powerfully assisted individuals in articulating policy opinions congruent with their personal material interests, the notable exception being among a small group of high-income people who became prompted to voice opposition.

The EITC presents a different set of results than the upwardly distributive policies, as shown in figure 3.4. In this case, all three income groups followed similar patterns, increasing their support for the policy—which was already strong—after receiving information about its distributive effects. As we anticipated, support grew substantially among both low-income subjects (from 55 to 81.4 percent) and middle-income subjects (from 63.2 to 81.6 percent) when they learned about the EITC's downwardly distributive tilt. Remarkably, those with high incomes also grew more favorable, with support increasing from 52.5 to 61.2 percent—nearly as much as their level of opposition, which rose from 15.3 to 26.6 percent.[48]

How can we explain why in each of these cases, some affluent individuals responded to new information by taking a position that would appear

FIGURE 3.3. Effects of Full Information on Views of Retirement Savings Contribution Tax Credit, by Income Group (%)

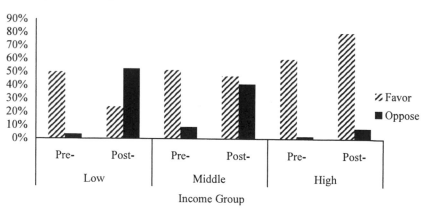

Source: Time-Sharing Experiments for the Social Sciences 2008, Mettler-Guardino Study.

FIGURE 3.4. Effects of Full Information on Views of Earned Income Tax Credit, by Income Group (%)

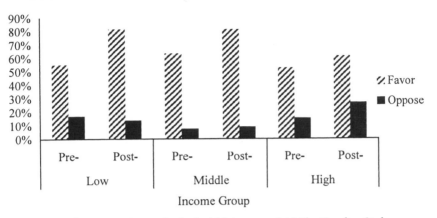

Source: Time-Sharing Experiments for the Social Sciences 2008, Mettler-Guardino Study.

to contradict their own self-interest, favoring instead that of the less fortunate? This finding is in accord with a recent study of public opinion by political scientists Benjamin I. Page and Lawrence R. Jacobs, which uncovered broad support—across income groups and partisan divides—for government programs that would reduce economic inequality. After respondents in a 2007 survey that Page and Jacobs conducted were informed with a description about who is aided by the EITC ("a program that helps working families who have low wages by reducing their income taxes or giving them refunds"), 68 percent—including majorities of Republicans and high earners—said that it should be expanded.[49] In fact, in the contemporary American polity, income is not a uniformly strong predictor of partisanship among the affluent.[50] Examining the high-income respondents in our study in terms of partisanship and ideology, we observe that many identify with or lean toward the Democratic Party (47 percent) and/or consider themselves liberal (38.4 percent). Such individuals, once informed of policy effects, were inclined to articulate policy preferences that favored the interests of the less well-off. The EITC, moreover, has also found support among some conservatives, who consider it a more palatable means of aiding the poor than public assistance, given that it explicitly rewards people for work. This may explain why among the high-income individuals who learned about the distributive effects of this tax credit, majorities of both Republicans and conservatives expressed support.

This leads to the question of whether policy-specific information enables individuals to formulate views that cohere with their ideological and political values. Using statistical analysis, we found that once individuals were informed of who benefits from the policies, Democrats and liberals became significantly more likely to oppose the upwardly distributive ones. The opportunity to learn about the impact of tax policies helped people to express positions that square with their underlying value orientations.

In sum, our experimental evidence indicates that policy-specific information can play a powerful role in facilitating opinion expression and meaningful change. Provision of clear and concise information helps citizens to articulate attitudes. New information partly mitigated the role of general political knowledge, enabling those less familiar with the political system to become more likely to express views. Distributive information in particular assists them in sensibly connecting their underlying interests and predispositions to opinions about typically hidden aspects of the federal tax code.

Adding further credibility to these findings, another experiment, conducted more recently than the one described here, offered a comparable test to our own and generated similar results. Political scientist John Sides found that when individuals are informed about who pays the estate tax—only about 1 percent of Americans—opposition to the tax declines and support grows. Sides went further, testing the impact of information alone and in combination with various rhetorical arguments, and found that its impact trumped anti-tax arguments.[51] His study lends credibility to the idea that actual information itself matters and can shift public opinion on policies that are usually incomprehensible to the public and that affect inequality. Sides's findings bolster the results of our experiment, suggesting that if simple information about the distributive effects of policies of the submerged state were widely available, public opinion toward its upwardly distributive elements would be considerably less favorable, while progressive policies that mitigate economic inequality would enjoy greater support.

Certainly these two experiments are only a start. As noted early in this chapter, we cannot know with certainty how experimental results compare to those that would be attained in the real world—a messy and noisy political milieu in which many citizens ignore political messages, their attention is fragmented, and multiple messages compete for their attention, some of which may tap sentiments such as partisan identity or ideology and thus gain more credence. Experimental findings acquire more credibility when subject to repeated trials, other variations are introduced, and real-world conditions are approximated through field experiments—all strategies that are well worth pursuing. We need to learn much more about how, in actuality, public policies influence citizens' engagement in democracy, in all of its manifestations.

Revealing Governance, Engaging Citizens

On a cold night in February 2008, I was driving home from work late and searching the radio for some news of the day. Suddenly, I heard the voice of then-candidate Barack Obama, speaking about the Home Mortgage Interest Deduction and explaining that it mostly benefits wealthy Americans. Fascinated, I froze the dial to listen: never before had I heard a political candidate speak about the policy's effects so clearly and forthrightly.

Then, I panicked: our experiment, described throughout this chapter, had just gone into the field! On that very night, individuals would be taking the Internet-based survey, telling us their views on the exact same policy of which this eloquent presidential candidate spoke. The timing of his speech might contaminate our results, ruining an experiment that Matt Guardino and I had spent a couple of years designing.

I need not have worried. I only happened to hear Obama speak about the Home Mortgage Interest Deduction because the satellite radio in that car picked up the POTUS (Politics of the United States) station, which is unusual in that it airs full speeches, unlike more high-profile media sources. Searching for days afterward, I found almost no mention in the mainstream media of Obama's unusually pointed discussion of what is typically a neglected and obscured topic.[52]

The idea that public policies should reflect the will of the majority of citizens is a basic principle of representative democracy. Yet in the case of the submerged state, many citizens lack basic information, and public officials fail to provide it, leaving the public unable to express its preferences in a meaningful way. Such policies have grown rapidly but largely out of public view, and thus many Americans tend to be unaware of how their basic features operate, not to mention who benefits from them. Yet, as this chapter has demonstrated with respect to tax expenditures, there is nothing intrinsically remote about such policies; rather, policymakers could reveal how they operate to the public by providing clear, simple, and straightforward information. Such information can serve as an important equalizing factor by enabling ordinary citizens to formulate meaningful views, the first step in becoming engaged as participants in the democratic process.

For American democracy to function and to thrive, it is not enough for public officials only to "nudge" citizens, as if the purpose of government is simply to foster social and economic outcomes desired by elites. Political leaders owe it to Americans to reveal to them the existence of the rapidly expanding policies of the submerged state, making it clear how they function and who benefits from them. Only if they are aware of the submerged state can people sensibly decide whether they support its uses of public resources, take a stand on them, and engage as citizens. Policy design, delivery, and publicity efforts can help to bridge the gap.

Now we will turn to policy developments during the Obama administration. Candidate Barack Obama set forth an ambitious agenda that required reconstituting key pillars of the submerged state. Would his administration manage to steer the nation toward a new politics, or would the usual patterns fostered by the submerged state—energized interests and passive publics—prevail? I will examine the extent to which Obama succeeded in the realms of higher education, tax expenditures, and health care, and why the record varied across the three. Drawing on the analysis in this chapter, I will explore the extent to which reformers managed to reveal the submerged state to citizens, either in the course of their efforts to date or in the design and delivery plans for policy achievements that will go into effect in the years to come.

4 · SCALING BACK
THE SUBMERGED STATE

The Victory for Student Aid

During the presidential campaign, candidate Barack Obama spoke out repeatedly about the need to broaden access to college and to restore the United States to its former position as the world's leader in college graduation rates. He vowed that if elected he would pursue these goals through a more generous and expansive student aid policy. Once he was in office, the overhaul of student aid, along with health care reform, rose to the top of the president's agenda. In April 2009 he offered a fiery speech that lambasted the bank-based system of student lending (Family Federal Education Loans, or FFEL) and clearly revealed the inner workings of the submerged state: "Under the FFEL program, lenders get a big government subsidy with every loan they make. And these loans are then guaranteed with taxpayer money, which means that if a student defaults, a lender can get back almost all of its money from our government. . . .Taxpayers are paying banks a premium to act as middlemen—a premium that costs the American people billions of dollars each year. . . . Well, that's a premium we cannot afford—not when we could be investing the same money in our students, in our economy, and in our country."[1]

Obama concluded by exposing the energized interest group politics fostered by this aspect of the submerged state. He took on the lenders directly, saying: "The banks and the lenders who have reaped a windfall from these subsidies have mobilized an army of lobbyists to try to keep things the way they are. They are gearing up for battle. So am I. They will fight for their special interests. I will fight for . . . American students and their families. And for those who care about America's future, this is a battle we can't afford to lose."[2] In this policy area, Obama consistently linked the demise of the submerged state to new policy efforts to mitigate inequality. He planned to use the savings from the termination of FFEL—the funds no longer siphoned off to lenders—to bolster other forms of student aid that could help increase the rate of college degree attainment:

more generous and dependable Pell Grants and funds for states and community colleges to foster student readiness and degree completion.

Opponents portrayed what was at stake in the politics of student aid in starkly different terms than Obama. They depicted the quest to eliminate lender subsidies and shift entirely to direct lending as a "government takeover." They warned that such a change would undermine "choice and competition" and lead to deteriorating customer service for student borrowers and higher costs for taxpayers.[3] As one Republican staffer put it, "It would make the U.S. Department of Education one of the ten largest banks in the country, but [Secretary] Arne Duncan is not a banker."[4]

Nonetheless within a year, Obama had triumphed over the bankers: tucked into the same 2,309-page reconciliation bill that included health care reform, lawmakers included provisions that ended the student loan system that had functioned through subsidies to lenders, and replaced it entirely with direct lending by government. It was an extraordinary accomplishment, one culminating over two decades of efforts by reform-minded policymakers. For Obama, it amounted to a signature achievement, one in which his administration's ambitious reach was well matched by its grasp. More broadly, it symbolized an extremely rare political event: the destruction of an established component of the submerged state.

Yet even this victory over hidden governance in student aid policy garnered little of the attention that was its due. It was overshadowed in part by the fact that the new programs of visible student aid ended up amounting to less than reformers had expected to win, even at late stages in the legislative process. More surprisingly, reformers themselves neglected to fashion new policies in ways that would help reestablish the bond between citizens and government. They willingly agreed to establish direct lending through delivery mechanisms that bear resemblance to those of the old bank-based system, making government's role less than clear. In addition, in the stimulus bill Obama had succeeded in attaining vast new tuition tax credits that enlarge the submerged state dramatically and direct substantial funds to students from higher-income families.

Given what we have seen in earlier chapters about the usual formidable obstacles to reforming the submerged state, how is it that Obama managed to score a victory over it by toppling the bank-based lending system? Conversely, how can we understand the limits of his administration's record in revealing governance through student aid? This chapter grapples with these questions. It shows that a confluence of circumstances, culminating with the credit crisis, had weakened the previously indomitable interest groups representing lenders. This allowed reformers in 2009 and

2010 to defeat them—albeit narrowly, despite the precipitous loss in their power. Yet the expected fruit of that victory—enlarged forms of visible student aid—failed to materialize to the extent that reformers had hoped they would. In part, congressional rules, historical contingencies, and the political challenges facing new expansions of direct spending conspired against them. But, in addition, the Obama administration itself took the initiative to expand the submerged state, through the creation of new tuition tax credits. The chapter also illuminates the administration's surprisingly limited attention to revealing what was at stake to ordinary citizens, and its lack of effort to fashion new policies in a way that could make government's role more evident. In order to understand the paradox of opponents' charges of a "government takeover" in this issue area, we begin by tracing government's historic role in the development of higher education policy, generally, and student loan policy, in particular.

A Pioneer Turned Laggard

The U.S. government has promoted higher education through its policies since the founding era. From eighteenth-century land grants through the Morrill Acts of the late nineteenth century, it provided resources to states to promote the development of universities and colleges. By the mid-twentieth century, it began to offer tuition assistance directly to students. At first, only veterans received such aid, starting with the original G.I. Bill of 1944. Civilians were then included through the National Defense Education Act of 1958; the Higher Education Act of 1965, including student loans and work-study; and Pell Grants as established in 1972. As a result of these policies, in the decades after World War II, the United States led the world in the caliber of its universities and colleges and in its rates of educational attainment. Thirty years ago, 37 percent of 25- to 34-year-old Americans held four-year college degrees, a rate higher than in any other nation.[5]

In recent decades, however, progress flagged as policies no longer continued to expand access to higher education and as policymakers failed to respond accordingly. Tuition rose steadily, outpacing inflation and median household income. Average Pell Grants diminished in real terms: they had covered 80 percent of tuition at public universities in the mid-1970s, but by the start of this century covered only 40 percent; their coverage of tuition at private institutions sank from 40 to 15 percent.[6] As a result, though growing numbers of students started college, actual graduation rates stagnated. Among today's 25- to 34-year-old Americans, still only 39 percent hold four-year college degrees, barely more than their parents' generation. Meanwhile, ten other nations have surpassed the United States in college graduation rates.[7]

Making matters worse, America's inadequate system of student aid has meant that increasingly higher education exacerbates rather than mitigates economic inequality. This was not always the case: in the middle of the twentieth century, public policies enabled growing percentages of young people from low- to moderate-income backgrounds to go to college. By contrast, between 1980 and 2007, the percentage of college graduates from families in the bottom income quartile increased only from 6.5 to 9.8 percent, a net change of just over 3 percentage points, whereas among those from families in the top quartile, rates soared from 33.6 to 75.9 percent, a whopping 42.3 percentage point increase. Among those in the second and third quartiles, progress was also less than impressive in both absolute and relative terms, growing to 18.3 and 33.4 percent, respectively.[8]

Throughout the 2008 presidential campaign, Obama—who is well aware of these trends—continually stressed the need to make college more affordable and accessible and to boost graduation rates. Campaigning in Iowa, he announced that if elected, he would aim to "put a college education within reach of every American."[9] Later, in his first speech as president to a joint session of Congress, he proclaimed: "By 2020, America will once again have the highest proportion of college graduates in the world."[10] Achieving these goals would be no small task, however, not least because existing policies had unintentionally fostered the development of the powerful student loan lobby, ready to marshal its forces to defend the status quo.

Entrenchment of the Submerged State

Since the 1980s, policymakers in an increasingly polarized Congress found it difficult if not impossible to agree on raising benefits in Pell Grants or on any other strategies to improve visible forms of student aid. The dominant approach instead became the route offered by the submerged state: they embraced student loans. Loans represented a "path of least resistance," because it was much easier to raise borrowing limits and to ease lending restrictions than to agree on new commitments of direct spending, and the subsidies for lenders lacked comparable visibility.[11] As a result, loans replaced grants as the prominent source of student aid; by 2009 the average undergraduate completed her studies $24,000 in debt.[12] Notably, loans function poorly as a tool to expand access to college to those who are less well-off since such individuals encounter greater difficulty gaining approval to borrow and have been less willing to do so.[13] The primary beneficiaries of the trend toward lending were not students but banks and other lenders, who found it to be an increasingly lucrative business.

By the late 1980s, however, policymakers in both parties had become disturbed about the growing profits accrued to lenders. Such rewards had never been imagined when policymakers established guaranteed student loans in 1965 and Sallie Mae in 1972. As the nation's deficits grew, an official in the George H. W. Bush administration hatched the idea of replacing FFEL with direct lending by government as a means to avoid paying hefty fees to banks. A bipartisan group of members of Congress began to promote the idea, managing to achieve a pilot program in the 1992 Higher Education Act reauthorization.

When Bill Clinton was elected president, he made one of his initial goals the complete replacement of bank-based lending with direct lending. Suddenly, the terms of the battle changed dramatically, and lenders themselves mobilized politically to protect the system that had benefited them so well. The Consumer Bankers Association brought representatives from banks all over the nation to Capitol Hill to lobby, and Sallie Mae launched a public relations campaign.[14] After a contentious fight, Congress adopted a weakened version of Clinton's plan, permitting the adoption of direct lending on only a limited basis.

Once Republicans took control of both chambers of Congress in 1995, members of both parties became more sharply polarized in their positions on student loans. As recently as the 1980s, most Republicans had expressed only tepid support for the policy, viewing the subsidies as unnecessary government spending.[15] By the late 1990s, however, they began to work in tandem with lenders, courting them as a source of campaign contributions while seeking rates and terms for them that would boost their profits.[16]

It was during this period that student loan companies reaped larger profits than ever, and they invested heavily in developing their political capacity. They created several new organizations based in Washington, D.C., to represent their interests and became intensely involved in campaign financing and lobbying. Sallie Mae established its PAC in the late 1990s; by 2008 it emerged as the top donor within the entire finance and credit industry, while fellow student lender Nelnet ranked ninth.[17] By 2007 Sallie Mae outspent all other finance and credit companies except Visa on lobbying; it devoted over $4 million to such activities, more than MasterCard, American Express, and many other major companies.[18] The industry gained loyal support from the new breed of Republican leaders who advocated for it and relied on its donations.

Throughout, student aid politics was dominated by fights over favorable rates and terms for lenders. It became increasingly clear that reformers could make little headway in pursuing expanded access to college until the existing student loan system was reconstituted. By the time Barack Obama became president, however, much had already begun to change.

Winds of Change

In 2006 the lenders' star, so long ascendant, began to fade. Investigative journalists exposed their stunning profits and the mutually supportive relationship between them and conservative politicians. In the midterm election, young people voted at their highest rates in many cycles, helping Democrats to take back control of both chambers of Congress. The victorious party took notice and prepared to respond to this constituency, early in 2007 introducing legislation that put lenders on the defensive.[19] New York Attorney General Andrew Cuomo launched his investigation into the lending practices of Sallie Mae and others, claiming that they maintained improper relationships with financial aid officers at institutions of higher education, to whom they offered perks in exchange for receiving "preferred lender" status.

Lenders may well have survived these blows were it not for the credit crisis that hit in 2008. Suddenly private sources of credit evaporated and Congress had to intervene to rescue the industry. It enacted the Ensuring Continued Access to Student Loans Act (ECASLA), authorizing the Department of Education to act as a secondary market that could buy FFEL loans from lenders and thus enable them to stay afloat.[20]

Only if the bank-based system was terminated would Obama be able to pursue his agenda of restoring American leadership in college graduation rates. By the time he was elected, it appeared that the lenders' dominance might be coming to an end and the way cleared for sweeping changes. The fragile foothold reformers had established when they created direct lending in 1993 had begun to emerge as the basis on which a more secure and fiscally responsible full system of student lending could be established.[21] Still, FFEL would not be terminated without a fight.

Countercurrent: Enlarging the Submerged State

Before commencing his efforts to transform student loans, Obama took action early in 2009 in the stimulus bill to increase dramatically tuition tax credits, a policy firmly ensconced within the submerged state. The American Opportunity Tax Credit, which Obama had championed throughout his campaign, differed in a few respects from the HOPE tax credits created under Clinton. Obama's advisers, who strongly endorsed tax expenditures, argued that his plan would aid more low-income people because even students from families with no tax liability could qualify for it and claim up to $1,000. Yet while HOPE had genuinely aided students from middle-class families, with eligibility capped at $48,000 for households with single earners and $96,000 for those with couples, Obama's tuition tax credit expanded coverage to more affluent households, with incomes of up to $90,000 and $180,000, respectively.[22] At a cost of $49 billion over ten years, it added a vast increase to the submerged state. In fact, in 2010, at $13.59 billion, it already cost 42 percent as much as the total spending for Pell Grants.[23]

Remarkably, despite the largesse offered through the American Opportunity Tax Credit, neither advocates for expanded access to higher education nor policy analysts greeted it with much enthusiasm. Similar policies have been found to have little or no impact on boosting college enrollment; they primarily just offset the tuition costs of those who would attend college regardless. In addition, some analysts worry that they may even have the perverse effect of encouraging colleges and universities to raise tuition.[24] Despite the refundability feature of Obama's plan, which might render it more available to less advantaged students, the fact that it is obtained only long after tuition is paid makes it unlikely to influence enrollment decisions, and thus it will probably be ineffective in expanding access to college. Moreover, because of its location in the tax system, citizens are unlikely to be very aware of its existence or effects.

Commencing the Fight for Direct Lending

When Obama placed student aid policy, along with health care reform, at the top of his domestic policy agenda for 2009, terminating the bank-based system of student loans figured centrally in his plans. His 2010 budget called for replacing it entirely with direct lending. He proposed to use the savings to make Pell Grants an entitlement and to index that program's benefit rates to the Consumer Price Index (CPI), as well as to provide funds to states and community colleges for initiatives aimed to improve graduation rates.

In an announcement that put wind into reformers' sails, the Congressional Budget Office released its official assessment of the cost savings that would be generated by the shift to direct lending. Whereas the White House had predicted that replacing FFEL would lower federal spending by $47 billion over ten years, the CBO projected that figure to be considerably larger, $87 billion.[25] At that juncture, even some who had waffled on the choice—such as those in trade organizations representing colleges and universities—added their voices to the growing chorus of support for the change. Through the summer of 2009, it appeared that the forces favoring the switch to direct lending clearly possessed the advantage.

In early July, Sallie Mae, Nelnet, and a few other large-volume, for-profit lenders put forward their own plan, claiming that it offered equivalent savings to the administration's approach. Acknowledging their lack of access to capital, the lenders' alternative actually eliminated their subsidies and required the federal government to take ownership of loans, as it did under ECASLA. At the same time, the plan retained a substantial role for the lenders—in loan origination, servicing, and collection—and mandated that government pay them fees for such activities.

The lenders' alternative garnered strikingly little support. It neglected to incorporate the concerns of smaller nonprofit lenders, which are far more widely distributed across the nation than Sallie Mae and Nelnet. In addition, it failed to satisfy congressional Republicans because it did not originate with private capital but with government. From their perspective, it amounted to a "bloated direct loan program," with the added expense of fees paid to lenders.[26] Democratic Representative George Miller, chairman of the House Education and Labor Committee repudiated the plan, saying, "It's unfortunate that a small number of lenders are using legislative gimmicks to mask the fact that their proposal would divert $15 billion into their own pockets at the expense of students."[27]

The lenders' weak position permitted the proponents of direct lending to take charge at this stage. By late July, Miller introduced legislation modeled on Obama's plans, calling for an end to the bank-based lending program and using the savings for Pell Grants, community colleges, and other programs geared to help students. The proposal sailed through committee, and by September was voted on and approved by the full House in the form of the Student Aid and Fiscal Responsibility Act (H.R. 3221, which became known as "SAFRA") by a vote of 253–171, along partisan lines with only a few exceptions.[28]

In a marked divergence from usual submerged state politics, no member of either party introduced a substitute amendment representing either the lenders' alternate proposal or any other viable approach to retain their role in student lending. Certainly plenty of rhetoric defended the existing system. As articulated by Republican John Kline (MN):

> The speed with which the Democrats are orchestrating a full government takeover of our classrooms and communities is astonishing. First, we saw a drive toward complete government takeover of our nation's health care system. Now we see government seizing control of student lending, forcing the private sector out and welcoming a mountain of public debt. I'm almost afraid to ask: What part of our lives will be handed over to government next?[29]

Yet opponents of direct lending refrained from putting forward a serious alternative. In part this reflected the Republicans' strategy in 2009–10 of unwillingness to compromise on issues generally. In addition, it revealed the practical impossibility, given the financial crisis, of creating a feasible alternative to direct lending that both originated with private capital and that offered government cost savings.[30]

SAFRA mandated the end of FFEL, no longer permitting lenders to originate loans, though it did allow them to compete to service them. It used the projected savings of $40 billion to do most of what the Obama administration had proposed with the exception of endowing Pell Grants with entitlement status. Pell Grant levels had already been increased in the stimulus bill, and growing demand for them during the recession exacerbated the fiscal challenges involved in converting them to entitlement status.[31] Rather, lawmakers adopted an approach that retained some discretion for budget appropriators while setting up benefits to increase annually at the rate of the CPI plus 1 percent. The legislation also included funds for community colleges: $10 billion for the American Graduation Initiative, which aimed to elevate the number of graduates by five million as of 2020; plus an expansion of the already existing College Access Challenge Grant Program, which awards grants to individual colleges and states that put forward innovative approaches to elevating enrollment and graduation rates.[32]

The speedy passage of SAFRA might make it seem that policymakers' concerted action to terminate major components of the submerged state is an unremarkable, everyday event. This is hardly the case. SAFRA only passed easily in the House because of the large majority of Democrats, the rules followed by the chamber, and the exceptional weakness of the lenders in 2009, when their economic and political strength was all but decimated by the credit crisis. Greater complications arose, as we shall see, once it was the Senate's turn to act.

The Lenders Fight Back

As early as the spring of 2009, a few Democrats in the Senate had signaled their opposition to the termination of the bank-based system. Senator Ben Nelson from Nebraska, home of the lender Nelnet, said, "I think it would be the wrong direction for people to outsource jobs from Lincoln, Nebraska, to Washington, D.C." Nelnet employed a thousand people in Lincoln and had consistently been among Nelson's most generous campaign donors over the previous five years.[33] Senator Blanche Lincoln of Arkansas also expressed concerns about potential job losses in her state.[34] Such defections among the Democrats spelled trouble for Obama's agenda. The party's caucus controlled sixty votes at most through 2009, but without being able to count on all of them and with no Republicans endorsing direct lending, the minority party could easily threaten a filibuster and prevent legislation from coming to the floor for a vote.[35]

Democratic leaders in the Budget Committees of both chambers had already foreseen this possibility and prepared a contingency plan. Senate rules permit one budget reconciliation vote per session, in which a simple majority of fifty-one—unstoppable by filibuster—may approve legislation that is strictly related to the budget. In April 2009, congressional leaders planned for the administration's direct lending proposal to be included in such a bill.[36] They placed "reconciliation instructions" in the compromise budget outline, requiring the committees responsible for education policy to reduce program spending by $1 billion or more.[37] Once the autumn arrived, it became apparent that they might ultimately need to combine elements of the higher education policy with health care reform in such a bill, so they put off action on the former while attempting to move forward on the latter, the president's top priority.

Lenders used the delay to organize the opposition, both at the grassroots and elite levels. Sallie Mae mobilized workers and residents in towns where it employs the greatest numbers. In Fishers, Indiana, over eighty-one thousand individuals signed a petition urging Congress to preserve a role for lenders. At a rally of company employees, hundreds of whom donned matching T-shirts that read "Protect Indiana Jobs," Sallie Mae CEO Albert Lord attempted to stir populist anger, declaring, "There's Washington, and then there's the rest of the country. This is the rest of the country."[38] Meanwhile, in Washington, D.C., lenders aimed to enlist five moderate

Democratic senators in support of retaining the FFEL program, spending millions on lobbying for that purpose.[39] Sallie Mae alone devoted over $4 million to such activities in 2009, the second-largest amount it had ever spent in one year.

By November the lenders appeared to be gaining ground: analysts predicted that Obama's proposal lacked the support of enough senators to pass.[40] The next month, Democratic Senator Bob Casey from Pennsylvania led eleven other moderate Democrats in support of an alternative to the House bill that would allow lenders to continue to originate government-backed loans and to be awarded fees by the federal government for doing so.[41] The prospects for the achievement of Obama's goals looked increasingly dismal. In keeping with the politics of the submerged state, vested interests were clearly abreast of what was at stake in reform efforts. From the point of view of most citizens, however, developments occurred well below the radar.

Mobilizing for Reform

Certainly mobilization did occur on behalf of reform efforts. While lenders worked in opposition to the student aid bill, the two membership organizations that address such issues, the Public Interest Research Group (PIRG) and the United States Student Association (USSA), worked vigilantly to promote it. As the financial crisis brought state budget cuts for public universities and colleges, these organizations found their memberships energized. The leadership of both had spent years aiming to replace FFEL with direct lending; the embodiment of that goal combined with improved student aid in the 2009–10 legislation made it a focal point for mobilizing their grassroots. And as one leader put it, "Students have been waiting for a while to get behind something they felt would impact them directly."[42]

The student organizations coordinated an impressive amount and variety of grassroots activity. During one week in September, US PIRG and its member groups around the nation collected petitions from students indicating the amount of debt they would have accumulated once they graduated; they displayed the amounts on bricks in a "Wall of Debt" that powerfully depicted the issues students faced. In October PIRG, USSA, and other associations united forces for a "Raising Pell" Week of Activism, in which they used social networking sites to reach students and mobilized them to take part in a national youth call-in and fax-in to the Senate, demanding the passage of SAFRA. The student organizations generated heightened activity particularly in states in which senators were considered swing votes, often because the student loan industry employed residents. The groups helped stimulate the publication of newspaper editorials in numerous locations and organized a financial aid hearing with Senator Casey in Pennsylvania. These organizations not only activated students but also coordinated their efforts with labor organizations, including the AFL-CIO and SEIU, and with civil rights organizations such as the NAACP and La Raza.[43]

Under the Radar

In 2010, as we will see, the underdog membership groups PIRG and USSA ultimately triumphed over the banks, yet neither possessed sufficient size to expose the reform of the submerged state to a significant portion of the American public. Whereas labor unions claim 12 percent of the workforce among their members, the organizations representing students speak for only a sliver of the public by comparison.[44] While access to college is an issue that concerns a wide swath of the population, not just those presently enrolled in higher education, no large federated membership organization speaks for citizens generally on the issue.

It was the president, having the power of the "bully pulpit," who stood poised to communicate to Americans broadly about the efforts to reform student aid, revealing to them what was at stake in the proposed transformation to direct lending. To assess the extent to which Obama addressed the issue, I conducted an analysis of all of the speeches, press conferences, and weekly addresses he gave on the subject between his Inauguration in January 2009 through March 2010. I did the same for tax policy and health care reform, both of which will be addressed in the next chapter. As seen in figure 4.1, Obama discussed student aid policy rarely compared to the other subjects: he spoke about it publicly only nine times during his first fourteen months in office, compared to sixty-eight times for health care and thirty-eight for taxes.[45] On some of those occasions, he focused on the topic for an entire speech, but on others it consumed only a few sentences in the midst of a press conference.

Examining Obama's statements on each topic, I also analyzed the frequency with which he "revealed the submerged state," meaning that he spoke frankly about how programs functioned and who benefited, in ways similar to those in the experiment described in chapter 3. Speeches containing such content are indicated by the lined sections of bars; the first speech, given in April 2009, is quoted in the opening paragraphs of this

FIGURE 4.1. Frequency of Obama's Public Statements on Social Welfare Issues: Revealing the Submerged State, February 2009–March 2010

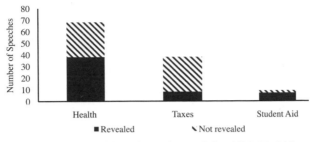

Source: Author's content analysis of "Speeches and Remarks" and "Weekly Addresses" by President Barack Obama, available at White House Briefing Room website, http://www.whitehouse.gov/briefing-room. See text and notes for discussion of coding guidelines.

FIGURE 4.2. Obama's Public Statements on Student Aid Policy: Revealing the Submerged State, February 2009–March 2010

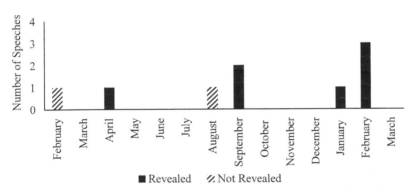

Source: Author's content analysis of "Speeches and Remarks" and "Weekly Addresses" by President Barack Obama, available at White House Briefing Room website, http://www.whitehouse.gov/briefing-room. See text and notes for discussion of coding guidelines.

chapter. As seen in figure 4.2, on the occasions that the president did talk publicly about student aid policy, he quite often explicitly revealed the submerged state—on seven out of nine occasions.[46] Figure 4.1 shows that he clearly described what was at stake in a far higher proportion of speeches on higher education than he did in his statements on health care reform or taxes. Yet because he spoke about it so infrequently and it was vastly overshadowed by the focus on health care, few Americans likely realized that the issue was under consideration, not to mention what was at stake in the outcome.

The Home Stretch

While the lenders and students mobilized and the public remained largely quiescent, in the Senate chamber the student aid bill remained on hold. Democratic leaders, who in early fall had been fairly confident that a bill could gain approval quickly through normal voting procedures, grew less certain as the months dragged on. Finally on December 24 the Senate approved a health care bill by the requisite sixty votes, and Congress recessed for the holidays. As 2010 began, Democrats prepared for final votes by each chamber on health care, and it seemed that student aid policy would soon have its own moment.

Then in the special Massachusetts Senate election on January 19, Republican Scott Brown surprised the nation and won the seat held for the past forty-seven years by the late Ted Kennedy—lifelong champion of health care reform, higher education and K–12 education policy, and other forms of social provision. Brown's victory terminated the Democrats' filibuster-proof majority in the Senate, upending the current legislative plans for completing votes on health care reform and also, therefore, for the student aid bill. Although leaders had long envisioned the possibility of combining the two issues in the reconciliation process as a last resort, the manner in which to pursue that approach was anything but clear.

Obama himself held firm to his position favoring direct lending, though the issue remained vastly overshadowed by the attention to health care reform. In the State of the Union address, in urging the Senate to follow the lead of the House on the issue, he offered one of his pointed statements that revealed what was at stake in the transformation to direct lending.

> To make college more affordable, this bill will finally end the unwarranted taxpayer subsidies that go to banks for student loans. Instead, let's take that money and give families a $10,000 tax credit for four years of college and increase Pell Grants.[47]

Combining two major policies into one legislative package presented challenges, however, despite the fact that it would lower the hurdle for approval in the Senate from sixty to fifty-one votes. For one thing, Democratic leaders in the House knew that the chances for another passage of a health care bill in the chamber had grown more difficult given the shift in the political winds and the fact that many members disliked features of the Senate version on which they would have to vote. In combining the issue with student aid legislation, they risked losing the support of their

own members who favored health care reform but opposed direct lending, such as Paul Kanjorski of Pennsylvania, in whose district Sallie Mae
employed many.

In addition, the CBO announced a new 2010 budget score for the student aid component that assessed its savings to be drastically lower than
estimated in 2009, $61 billion instead of $87 billion. The lower score owed
in part to the fact that over the past year, given the circumstances of the
credit crisis and urging from officials in the U.S. Department of Education, a large number of universities and colleges had already voluntarily
moved to adopt direct lending. This meant that much of the projected
savings from the shift had already been realized—in effect, an unheralded
success. In addition, the recession had prompted soaring college enrollments and more students than ever qualifying for Pell Grants, which in
turn created vastly greater costs for that program.[48] If Congress utilized
the CBO's reduced assessment of savings, it would mean substantially less
money could be used for new spending for students.

At this juncture, the fate of the student aid legislation fell to Senate Budget Committee Chair Kent Conrad, who possessed the authority to deem
whether its provisions met the special criteria for its inclusion in the reconciliation package. Conrad, in whose state student lending by the Bank
of North Dakota provided a significant number of jobs and revenues,
had never been a supporter of direct lending.[49] He could now determine
whether proposed legislation met the twin criteria of, first, funding only
existing programs, not new ones; and second, achieving overall budgetary
savings. His initial assessment was that the student aid provisions should
not be combined in the package with health care reform. Upon hearing this
news, advocates for the higher education provisions were stunned: they
believed the legislation would die if delayed beyond the midterm elections.
In meetings of the Democratic Caucus, Senator Tom Harkin, chair of the
Senate HELP Committee, and Chairman Miller offered impassioned pleas
for the inclusion of the provisions. Yet even at this stage, six moderate Democratic senators sent a letter expressing their concerns that the termination
of FFEL would bring job losses to their states.[50] Conrad finally conceded to
include the higher education provisions, but in a decision that infuriated
other Democrats, he insisted on using the new lower 2010 CBO score for
cost savings, which meant tens of billions less available for student aid.

Moreover, the health care bill on its own did not provide sufficient savings to be considered revenue-neutral; the projected cost savings from the
student aid legislation enabled it to be enacted through reconciliation procedures by meeting the necessary requirements.[51] Therefore, of the $61 bil-

lion in estimated savings from loan reform, the leadership requested $9 billion to help finance health care reform and $10 billion for deficit reduction. These changes left $43 billion—less than half of what policymakers had expected as recently as one month earlier—for the creation and expansion of visible programs to promote access to college and to elevate completion rates.

In the final days before the legislation came to a vote, as policymakers wrangled over how the remaining funds would be allocated, organizations representing four-year institutions—which prioritized Pell Grant funding—exercised a far more audible voice in the process than the community college sector. Ultimately, the Pell Grants provision included neither Obama's wish for an entitlement guarantee nor the House plan for annual increases at the rate of inflation plus 1 percent, but rather only the requirement of increases at the rate of inflation. Maximum levels of such grants were set to increase gradually from $5,550 for the next two years up to $5,975 in 2020—a significant change, but far less than the rate of $6,900 the House had approved in SAFRA.[52] In a crushing defeat for community colleges, negotiators—bowing to Conrad's objections that it was a new program and failed to meet reconciliation criteria—cut Obama's signature American Graduation Initiative. The final bill included only $2 billion for such purposes, channeled through an existing program created by the stimulus bill. As in the House bill, $2.55 billion was included for minority-serving institutions, with whom lenders had long-established close ties; such funds had been seen as necessary to secure the support of the Congressional Black Caucus.[53]

Viewed in light of the power that student lenders had long enjoyed on Capitol Hill, the termination of the bank-based system, which had been such an established part of the submerged state, attracted remarkably little attention as the reconciliation legislation proceeded through final passage. On close inspection, however, Obama's victory for student aid was by no means a foregone conclusion. When the Senate voted, three Democrats— Nelson, Pryor, and Lincoln, each of whom had voted in favor of health care reform in December—opposed the reconciliation bill, once the student aid provisions were attached. Each was known to be a defender of the existing student loan system and an opponent of the shift to direct lending. The legislation passed by a final vote of only 56–43, a margin that would not have withstood a filibuster if it occurred outside reconciliation procedures. Remarkably, even at a point in time after the corrupt practices of the student loan industry had been well exposed, at a juncture when the credit crisis had rendered FFEL untenable without what amounted to a substantial government bailout, nonetheless the shift to direct lending had barely succeeded. In essence, like an exception that illustrates the rule, the demise of bank-based lending demonstrates that only under extraordinary circumstances is it possible to terminate key components of the submerged state, particularly given that the vast majority of citizens remain largely incognizant of the significance of such changes.

After the House approved the bill in a vote of 220–211 near midnight on March 21, and the Senate followed a few days later, the historic nature of the health care provisions overshadowed the student aid achievements. Yet the end of FFEL culminated a battle that had begun more than two decades earlier, finally terminating the system that had privileged and empowered lenders more than students. The savings, though less than reformers had hoped for, was directed to programs that would help less advantaged Americans attend college and complete degrees. As one staffer put it, "We have taken money from a vested interest and given it to some of the most low-income people in our country. We don't do that very often."[54] On March 30, at Northern Virginia Community College, President Obama signed the new bill into law.

Cloaking Visible Governance

The termination of bank-based student lending and its replacement by 100 percent direct lending represent the most significant shift from submerged to visible governance achieved by Obama to date. It was made possible by the credit crisis, which had devastated the capacity of the lenders to make a plausible case that their role contributed in any way to economic efficiency. Their defenders on Capitol Hill found it impossible to design an alternative that preserved the lenders' role and simultaneously featured cost savings. Even with their power seemingly so decimated, however, the lenders could still have prevailed had not Democratic leaders possessed the foresight to plan for the provision's placement in the reconciliation package, and had not one senator—Budget Committee Chair Kent Conrad—ultimately acquiesced to their inclusion at final passage. In other words, even in a position of relative weakness, the interest groups empowered by the submerged state still nearly managed to retain their privileged position.

In keeping with the traditional quiescence of the public in the politics of the submerged state, few citizens seemed aware of the battles or of what was at stake. Although Obama's speeches on the issue ably demonstrated that he could easily explain what was involved, they were few and far between. Preoccupied with health care reform, the president refrained from actively rallying the public on student aid. The student organizations did their best to mobilize their members, but those efforts reached only a narrow slice of the public.

To what extent will citizens become aware of government's role now that student lending will be administered by the U.S. Department of Education? While one might assume that the public provision of loans would be made obvious, the answer is not so clear. Throughout the legislative process, department officials, seeking to quell the voices of critics, had emphasized that under direct lending, the private sector would continue to perform several roles. The administration promised that the federal government would use "competitive Treasury auctions to acquire capital for student loans from private investors" and that the disbursement, servicing, and collection of loans would be carried out through a "competitive contracting process."[55] Notably, in the final bill Obama signed into law, $1.5 billion was set aside for loan servicing by the same companies that had long benefited from the profits that FFEL had made possible.[56]

In fact, proponents of direct lending themselves seemed inattentive to the broader significance of the change and its implications for citizens' experience of government. Explaining how the delivery of direct lending would compare to that of bank-based student loans, one Department of Education official noted: "From the customer perspective, it will not be very different—students will barely know the difference. It is a government program, like before, and run by private actors, like before."[57] With the department contracting out the originating and servicing of the loans, student borrowers may continue to have little awareness that government itself is aiding them in attaining their college degrees. As a result, they may be nearly as unlikely to understand the role of public policy in student aid or to become engaged in politics as a result.

The same is likely true of the beneficiaries of the American Opportunity Tax Credit, to which the administration has devoted such considerable resources. Individuals who benefit from such policies, unlike those who use more visible programs like Pell Grants and the G.I. Bill, are less likely to consider themselves to have benefited from government, and thus they are less likely to participate at higher rates in politics subsequently.[58]

In the realm of student aid, Obama had managed to claw back a significant portion of the submerged state, yet that victory—though roundly criticized by opponents—was barely noticed by the general public, which should have been supportive. The administration itself helped ordain such an outcome. It had neglected the opportunity to make citizens well aware of what was happening while it was in progress and to endorse them as supporters. Neither did administration officials set up the new direct lending program to ensure that Americans affected by it would notice government's role going forward. Meanwhile, Obama had actually expanded the submerged state through innovations in tuition tax credits.

In terms of the impact on inequality, ultimately the defeat of the lenders does not in and of itself promise higher college graduation rates for less well-off Americans. The improvements in Pell Grants and aid for community colleges that Obama had intended to accompany it—funds that could help facilitate that outcome—ended up being much less than hoped for. The new tuition tax credits, moreover, may do more to exacerbate inequality than to lessen it. Significantly, however, the new law promises over time to transform the landscape of student aid politics: no longer will it be dominated by the lenders, with their demands for more favorable subsidies and terms. Going forward, that change may enable policymakers to put students' needs first and foremost.

5 · SUSTAINING AND EXPANDING THE SUBMERGED STATE

Tax Policy and Health Care Reform

After intense and protracted battles over health care reform throughout most of 2009, on Christmas Eve the Senate approved legislation by the requisite sixty votes to prevent a filibuster. As Congress adjourned for the holidays, proponents of reform in Washington, D.C., breathed a sigh of relief, believing that a signing ceremony would soon be in order. But in mid-January, as policymakers readied for final votes in each chamber on a merged bill, suddenly everything changed. When Republican candidate Scott Brown won an upset victory over Democrat Martha Coakley in the special election for the Massachusetts Senate seat, it ended the Democrat's filibuster-proof majority, tearing asunder the plans for the law's final enactment. It also symbolized, to many, a mid-course, popular referendum on Obama's reform agenda.

During the long months while interest groups had lobbied aggressively on health care policy and political elites had negotiated, maneuvered, and cut deals, ordinary citizens increasingly perceived themselves to be cut out of the loop. Members of the public who just fifteen months earlier had rallied behind candidate Barack Obama—believing him to be the agent for change who could transcend "politics as usual" and bring the needs of the people to the fore—had grown either complacent or, worse, restive. Asked to explain her vote for Scott Brown, lifelong Democrat Marlene Connolly of North Andover, Massachusetts, said, "I voiced my opinion and voted for a Republican, and the roof did not cave in. I can't believe I'm saying this . . . but I think I am now a Republican. I'm just devastated by what Obama's doing. I don't think he cares enough about anything other than his own personal agenda or this foolish health care bill. . . . It bothered me very much that it's Kennedy's seat, that did bother me. But the health bill totally upsets me. First of all, do we really know what's going on with it? It's always evasive when they're talking about it."[1]

Brown's startling victory represented a public backlash against the politics of the submerged state, against the manner in which even efforts to reform it revolved around elites and organized interests, leaving the public feeling confused and excluded, their pressing needs seemingly forgotten. Throughout 2009, ordinary Americans could not help but see the mobilization of powerful interest groups and the fact that many of their demands were accommodated through the political process. A poll in October asked respondents how much of the blame for the difficulty in passing health care reform legislation was attributable to "special interest groups such as big pharmaceutical and health insurance companies." Fully 49 percent answered "a great deal," and 26 percent said "quite a bit"; only 15 percent said "very little," and 5 percent, "none at all."[2] A few months later, pollsters talked to individuals who opposed the health care proposals being discussed in Congress. They asked them the extent to which their stance could be explained as "too much of the process took place behind closed doors and involved too much deal-making." Seventy-three percent responded that this was the "major reason" for their opposition; only 18 percent said it was a "minor reason," and 8 percent said it was "not a reason."[3]

Yet while citizens rightly perceived that the legislative process had been heavily influenced by vested interests in the health care arena, they had gained little understanding of what the policy might do for them and their families—indeed, most lacked confidence that it would be of any help. Repeatedly, when pollsters asked Americans whether the "new health care reform bill will mostly help you personally, will mostly hurt you personally," or whether it would not have "much of an effect on you personally," only 17 percent said they believed it would help them, 36 percent said it would hurt them, and 39 percent anticipated no effect.[4] Even when the law was finally passed in March 2010, surveys revealed that Americans knew little about its contents and that a large portion of the public said they disapproved of it—despite the fact that when people were asked about their views of particular provisions that happened to be included, the majority repeatedly voiced support for them.

This chapter examines the politics of both health care reform and tax breaks during the first two years of Obama's presidency. In the realm of student lending, as shown in the previous chapter, the credit crisis and other factors had dramatically weakened the power of the lenders and lawmakers' views about the feasibility of the bank-based system. In the health care and tax arenas, by contrast, the industries subsidized by the submerged state continued to wield considerable power. The Obama administration could not make headway, therefore, unless it managed to negotiate successfully with these key players. It had to set its sights not on replacing the existing system but rather on restructuring it and building upon it. As we will see, the president met with insurmountable opposition in his efforts to scale back existing tax breaks for the wealthiest Americans, but in health care reform, remarkably, he found success.

Once again, however, the results of reform efforts eluded much of the public, and even more than in the case of student aid, the process and policy outcomes left people confused and alienated. Despite the fact that after a momentous political struggle Obama ultimately derived victory in health care reform, few Americans were convinced of its value for them. Similarly, one-third of the stimulus bill consisted of tax breaks, but even one year after its enactment, few people were aware of them. Obama had addressed the issues of taxes and health care frequently in his public statements, but he rarely revealed how the submerged state functioned. Moreover, the reform process showcased the power of interest groups, and that proved off-putting to most Americans. Finally, the outcomes in each case actually enlarged the submerged state, at least in some of its components, thus making it difficult for citizens to recognize government's transformed role in their lives.

A full recounting of either the development of tax policy or of the tumultuous health care reform saga during Obama's first years in office lies beyond the scope of this book. The aim of this chapter, rather, is to explain the submerged state's role both in making these reform efforts so challenging and in undercutting public recognition of policy achievements.

Tax Expenditures

Although health care policy dominated the headlines during Obama's first year in office, tax policy figured even more centrally in his domestic agenda, not least for purposes related to social welfare. He looked to the tax code to accomplish a variety of goals: to reallocate broad priorities; to devote resources to an array of purposes; to mitigate rising economic inequality; and to raise revenues for health care reform.

During the presidential campaign, Obama articulated several goals linking tax policy and social welfare. He planned to allow the 2001 and 2003 Bush tax cuts to expire for affluent Americans, restoring the rates on high incomes, capital gains, and dividends that existed previously. He also sought to scale back the regressivity of tax expenditures that favored the wealthy. He planned to reinstate limits that had existed less than a decade earlier on the extent of personal exemptions and such itemized deductions as the Home Mortgage Interest Deduction and charitable contributions.[5] In 1990 a relatively unknown member of the House Ways and Means Committee named Donald Pease had inserted an obscure amendment into the budget reconciliation bill, one that lowered the value of itemized deductions for the most affluent households.[6] The bill, containing the Pease Amendment and also a "personal exemption phase-out" for households with the largest incomes, had been signed into law by President George H. W. Bush as part of a bipartisan-supported deficit-reducing measure. Just one decade later, those restrictions on tax breaks had been phased out, scheduled to terminate entirely by 2010, when George W. Bush signed into law the 2001 tax cuts.[7]

Obama also aimed to channel a higher proportion of tax expenditures to low- and moderate-income people, through both the creation of new policies and alterations to existing ones. During the 2008 campaign he said, "Today we have a mortgage interest deduction, but it only goes to people who itemize on their taxes. Like so much in our tax code, this tilts the scales to the well-off."[8] To address this and similar inequities, he planned to make new and existing tax breaks "refundable" so that even those with no tax liability could benefit from them.[9]

Expanding the Submerged State in the Stimulus Bill

When President Roosevelt took office in the midst of the Great Depression, his administration moved quickly to create expansive relief programs to employ millions of jobless Americans. Decades later, those individuals and their family members still recalled the help they had found through the Civilian Conservation Corps, the Civil Works Administration, and other initiatives.[10] Similarly, within five short weeks of taking office, President Obama scored several victories aimed at reviving a devastated economy. Most of them were packed together into the massive American Recovery and Reinvestment Act of 2009, otherwise known as the stimulus bill. Yet although this law resembled legislation enacted during Roosevelt's "First Hundred Days" both in its scope and purpose, it differed dramatically by making tax breaks the primary vehicle for offering relief to most Americans.

In total, tax breaks amounted to $288 billion, fully 37 percent of the entire $787 billion stimulus package.[11] The largest of these was the president's signature proposal, the Making Work Pay Tax Credit. It was based on principles like those of the Earned Income Tax Credit (EITC), but reached well up into the middle class: individuals with incomes up to $75,000 qualified for a credit of up to $400 and married couples with incomes up to

$150,000 qualified for a credit of up to $800. In addition, as we saw in the last chapter, the American Opportunity Education Tax Credit offered up to $2,500 to reimburse families for college tuition costs.[12] The bill also included several other tax features, including increases in the EITC and child tax credit; one-time payments of $250 to recipients of Social Security, SSI, Railroad Retirement, Veteran Disability Compensation, and some federal and state pensions; and tax credits of up to $8,000 for first-time home buyers.[13]

The stimulus bill achieved Obama's goals of channeling funds toward low- to moderate-income Americans, but it did so by further expanding the submerged state. In political terms, with more than one out of three dollars in the bill tucked into tax breaks rather than showcased in more obvious forms of social welfare such as relief payments or job creation, it was not clear that Americans would clearly recognize the evidence of Obama's efforts. Indeed, as discussed earlier, one year later only 12 percent of Americans knew that taxes had been decreased under the Obama administration.[14] Although 95 percent of employed Americans owed less in taxes thanks to the tax credits in the stimulus, most were unaware of it. It offered a piercing contrast to the legacy of Roosevelt's relief policies, which are still evident, seventy-five years later, dotting the American landscape in the form of bridges, dams, reservoirs, and buildings and trails in the nation's park system.

Failing to Scale Back the Submerged State

The budget that President Obama presented to Congress in February 2009 contained nearly all of his campaign promises for changes in the tax code, including plans to scale back the regressivity of some tax expenditures. Attempting to reinstate provisions that the Bush tax cuts had dissolved, Obama proposed that affluent Americans in the top two tax brackets—36 and 39.6 percent—should have their deductions, such as those for home mortgage interest and charitable contributions, limited to their value at the 28 percent tax bracket.[15] Those two tax deductions are especially regressive: as we saw in chapter 1, in 2004 American families with incomes of $100,000 and above—just one out of seven households—claimed 69 percent of the subsidies for the Home Mortgage Interest Deduction; they also claimed 78 percent of those for the charitable contributions deduction.[16] Scaling back how much the wealthy could derive from these benefits would help to reduce inequality. The president planned to use the saved revenues—projected to amount to $267 billion over ten years—to help finance health care reform, for which they would provide approximately 45 percent of the needed funds.

On Capitol Hill, however, Obama's plan to curtail the sharp upward redistributive effects of these tax breaks met not only with antipathy from Republicans but also, more strikingly, from Democratic leaders. Among the members of the president's own party who offered a less-than-enthusiastic reception to the plan, House Majority Leader Democrat Steny Hoyer (MD) warned, "That's going to be controversial. And, obviously, charitable contributions . . . [present] great concern. Clearly, one of the greatest concerns will be very, very large-income donors who make very substantial contributions to very worthwhile enterprises."[17] Representative Charles Rangel, chair of the House Ways and Means Committee, also expressed reservations, noting, "I would never want to adversely affect anything that is charitable or good."[18] Senator Max Baucus (MT), chair of the Finance Committee, cautioned, "Some of the reforms and offsets . . . such as the limitations on itemized deductions, raise concerns and will require more study as we determine the best policies for getting America back on track."[19]

What could explain such swift stonewalling—even from fellow Democrats—to modifying these tax breaks for the wealthy? A compelling answer lies in the political force exerted by the organized groups that benefit from such provisions, starting with the real estate lobby. On the day Obama presented his budget, Charles McMillan, president of the National Association of Realtors, wrote to him opposing changes to the Home Mortgage Interest Deduction. He argued, "Diminishing or eliminating the [HMID] would hurt all families, the housing market, and our national economy. . . . [A]t a time when our housing and real estate markets are suffering, we believe it would be irresponsible for the real estate industry and federal policymakers to consider, much less support, any proposal seeking to alter the [HMID]."[20] The Realtors' organization circulated similar letters to all U.S. senators and representatives, and it also published ads expressing the same message in several newspapers.[21] The Financial Services Roundtable, Mortgage Bankers Association, and the National Association of Home Builders also quickly announced their antagonism toward any alterations to the real estate tax deductions.[22]

Such letters and ads carried weight because the real estate lobby had cultivated relationships with politicians from both parties over a long period of time. We already saw, in chapter 2, that the industry had contributed to campaigns at high levels, with an increasingly intense commitment of resources in recent years. In fact, overall it ranked among the most generous six industries in every electoral cycle since at least 1990. Moreover, its contributions were distributed widely: in 2008 the real estate industry donated to every single member of the U.S. House, giving $53,470 on average, and it donated to all but five senators, giving an average of $401,462. The National Association of Realtors alone spent $20 million on lobbying in 2009, making it the tenth biggest spender across all types of organizations in the nation; overall, the real estate industry devoted $65 million to lobbying that year.[23]

While it may come as little surprise that the real estate industry invested vast sums in self-interested political activity, remarkably the non-profits, foundations, and philanthropy sector—generally perceived as a beacon of altruism—behaved in a very similar manner. Because their activities account for a much smaller portion of GDP than the real estate industry, understandably charitable organizations spent considerably less on campaign contributions than the real estate sector in 2008—just one-eighth as much ($18 million). Strikingly, however, they committed fully two-thirds as much to lobbying in 2009—a total of about $44 million.[24]

Charitable organizations invested especially heavily in efforts to halt Obama's plans for changes in the tax code. A few philanthropists did express doubts that the proposed changes would affect the rate of charitable giving, predicting that any negative influence would be minor and far outweighed by the value of health care reform.[25] But major trade associations such as the Council on Foundations actively and successfully fought the Obama administration's proposals.[26] In effect, they provided policymakers with "cover" for opposing changes in tax deductions generally, enabling them to invoke the moral high ground associated with protecting the philanthropic sector, while simultaneously shielding the real estate industry as well. Their arguments quickly derailed the administration's primary plan for financing health care reform.

By late March, just one month after Obama introduced his proposal to modify the two especially regressive tax deductions, the Senate had already taken action to stymie it. At Baucus's urging, Democrats endorsed an amendment to the budget resolution offered by Republican Senator Bob Bennett (UT) requiring that health care not be funded by alteration of the tax benefits tied to charitable contributions.[27] A few weeks later, when the Senate Finance Committee released a report listing policy options for raising revenues to pay for health care reform, it offered no comment on the president's preferred approach.[28]

While the real estate industry and philanthropies had risen to the defense of existing arrangements, no broad-based membership groups put forth a countervailing argument on behalf of the general public or even an organized segment of it. Although the organizations that mobilized against the bank-based student loan system did not represent a vast portion of the American public, nonetheless they did make citizens' voices heard in the debate, as they countered the force of the lenders both on Capitol Hill and through grassroots organizing. In the realm of tax policy, by contrast, a comparable voice was completely missing from discussions in Washington, D.C., and no organization publicized the issue among citizens or mobilized them to take action.

In addition, because the Obama administration had sought to avoid the difficulties the Clinton administration encountered by letting Congress take the primary role in designing health care legislation, the president refrained from strongly promoting the financing plan he favored. During a prime-time news conference in March, a reporter asked him whether he regretted having advanced his plan of cutting back deductions for mortgages and charities. Obama answered forthrightly, "No, I think it's the right thing to do." Referring to the rise of economic inequality, he defended the approach as a way to "raise some revenues from people who benefitted enormously over the last several years." Then in a statement unusual for a political leader in its candor at revealing how an aspect of the submerged state functions, he explained:

> People are still going to be able to make charitable contributions. It just means if you give $100 and you're in this tax bracket, at a certain point, instead of being able to write off 36 (percent) or 39 percent, you're writing off 28 percent. Now, if it's really a charitable contribution, I'm assuming that that shouldn't be the determining factor as to whether you're giving that hundred dollars to the homeless shelter down the street. . . . What it would do is it would equalize. When I give $100, I get the same amount of deduction as . . . a bus driver who's making $50,000 a year or $40,000 a year [who] give[s] that same hundred dollars. Right now, he gets 28 percent—he gets to write off 28 percent, I get to write off 39 percent. I don't think that's fair.[29]

Yet never did Obama offer a major speech in which he explained to the American public with similar clarity how such policies work and what difference proposed changes would make and for whom. The president refrained from making a full and sustained case for the financing plans his administration put forward, and the public lacked opportunities to become informed. The issue thus remained largely invisible to citizens.

Without a concerted effort by the president to promote his progressive approach to financing health care reform and in the absence of public mobilization for it, the administration's plan continued to lose traction. In June the Senate Finance Committee considered a more modest version of Obama's proposal, one that would limit itemized deductions for the affluent to current tax rates—no more than 35 percent—even after the Bush-era tax cuts expired. Immediately, the executive directors of numerous philanthropic organizations wrote to Chairman Baucus expressing their opposition even to this scaled-down alternative. In a classic example of portraying an alteration of the submerged state as if it amounted to intervention in a freely functioning market, they wrote, "Both proposals, in essence, impose a tax on charitable giving."[30] In September committee member Jay Rockefeller (WV) made a last-ditch effort to promote the 35 percent limit, but none of his amendments made their way into the committee's final bill.[31] Still not convinced such proposals had died completely, Republicans rallied again in November when Senator John Thune of South Dakota and thirty others signed and circulated a "Dear Colleague" letter to the rest of the Senate, urging them to protect the "full value of the charitable deduction by opposing any amendments to the health care reform bill that impose a cap on itemized deductions."[32] Such efforts put a final nail in the coffin of Obama's plans for reducing the scope of these components of the submerged state that aid primarily the most affluent among American families.

Revealing Little

Given that the submerged state of tax expenditures is not visible to most Americans as it is to the interest groups that benefit from it, the task falls to reformers to reveal its key features to the public. An analysis of all speeches, press conferences, and weekly addresses given by Obama between his Inauguration in January 2009 through March 2010 shows that he spoke about taxes thirty-eight times. As seen in figure 5.1, taxes constituted a common theme in February 2009, when Obama spoke regularly about the tax breaks that were part of the stimulus.[33] After that, however, though the subject of taxes came up fairly often, it was in the context of speeches focusing on health care reform, and it took the form of brief comments about either financing or incentives and mechanisms through which the policy would operate. As indicated by the lined sections of the bars, furthermore, even direct references to taxes rarely involved statements that made explicit the actual features of the submerged state. Content analysis of the speeches

FIGURE 5.1. Obama's Public Statements on Tax Policy: Revealing the Submerged State, February 2009–March 2010

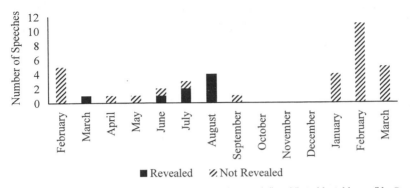

■ Revealed   ⁄⁄ Not Revealed

Source: Author's content analysis of "Speeches and Remarks" and "Weekly Addresses" by President Barack Obama, available at White House Briefing Room website, http://www.whitehouse .gov/briefing-room. See text and notes for discussion of coding guidelines.

revealed that on only eight of the thirty-eight occasions did the president actually describe how such policies functioned and who benefited. Such statements, moreover, were usually very brief: Obama's full statement from the March 2009 press conference quoted above, for instance, occupied only 446 words in the midst of a 9,000-word news conference.[34] Citizens had little opportunity to realize what was at stake.

By contrast, groups benefiting from existing arrangements continued to be astutely aware of developments and poised to act when necessary to protect the status quo. As 2009 came to a close, the National Association of Realtors applauded itself for effectively "protecting the mortgage interest deduction," noting that it had "aggressively fought off changes to the [HMID] through grassroots, advertising and similar advocacy tools."[35] Subsequently, reformers had to seek other means for financing health care reform, favoring alternatives that did not provoke the established groups that stood ready to refute changes to existing arrangements.

Obama had come into office with ambitious plans for reconstituting the hidden welfare state of tax expenditures and for undercutting its upwardly redistributive bias. His efforts to scale back the most generous tax breaks for the wealthy, however, foundered on the shoals of highly energized interests, the vast and deep political support they have cultivated among elected officials, and a quiescent public. Obama did succeed in his goal of creating expansive new tax breaks, but these policies add further to the size and scope of the submerged state and most of them do not effectively mitigate inequality. Most problematic, they are imperceptible to most Americans.

Health Care Reform

By 2008 policymakers widely agreed that the U.S. health care system was in crisis. Health care costs had climbed to 16 percent of GDP—more than the percentage spent in any other OECD nation and twice the spending of the average.[36] Although the United States has long been the only nation in the Western industrialized world that lacks national health insurance, the U.S. government spends substantially more than other countries on health care—especially on the subsidization of employer-provided health care, Medicare, and Medicaid.[37] These high costs notwithstanding, one in six Americans lacked health insurance at any point in time, and over the course of a two-year period, one in three people under age sixty-five went without insurance for at least part of the time.[38] The rates of un-insurance soared as the percentage of Americans with employer-provided private insurance benefits fell sharply, declining from 68 to 59 percent be-tween 2000 and 2009.[39] Those fortunate enough to have insurance faced troubles too, namely, soaring costs: between 1999 and 2008, the average amount families paid in health insurance premiums increased by 119 per-cent, while family income increased only by just 29 percent. Employers, meanwhile, struggled to pay their share, and many cut back on workers' pay increases or retirement contributions in order to keep up.[40]

As a result of these circumstances and the problems they presented to citizens and employers alike, health care reform hit the political agenda again in 2009 as it has approximately every fifteen years since 1920. Each time, the issue has consumed the attention of policymakers and the me-dia for months, and featured intense drama and deal-making between the political parties and with interest groups.[41] That embarking upon health care reform again would require Herculean efforts by the president and congressional leaders was a certainty; that such efforts would guarantee success was anything but. And yet in 2010 the reformers won.

As much or even more than other aspects of the submerged state, exist-ing arrangements for the health care system have long fostered powerful vested interests, complicating the quest for reform. Over the past decade, the amount that strictly health-related groups have spent on lobbying—$3.788 billion—ranked second only to what the finance, insurance, and real estate sector spent, and much of the lobbying by those industries—as well as by other miscellaneous business groups—also focused on health care.[42] And just as in the other areas of the submerged state, government's role in subsidizing private actors in the provision of health care remained largely hidden from ordinary citizens.

The Origins of Submerged Health Policy and Politics

Throughout the long history of struggles over health care reform in the United States, organized interests played leading roles—primarily as antagonists.[43] Time and again, they helped to thwart reform efforts. They used their access to policymakers in Washington, D.C., to exert their influence, and they employed advertising campaigns to instill worry among the public and to weaken public support for reform.

Such activism originated prior to the development of the submerged state and helped to foster its early development. The American Medical Association (AMA) opposed national health insurance as early as 1920 and impeded its inclusion in New Deal legislation.[44] Meanwhile, private insurance companies emerged during the Depression, initiated by the American Hospital Association (AHA), which sought stable sources of revenue for struggling community hospitals. Blue Cross, the predominant one, organized as a corporation in 1938, and the AHA successfully lobbied for its exemption from state-level taxation. Then the Internal Revenue Service followed suit and exempted Blue Cross insurance from federal taxes, adopting what became an important precedent.[45]

Two federal government policies established during World War II fortified the foundations of the submerged state in the health care arena. In 1942 Congress passed a Revenue Act that prohibited profiteering by companies during the war by imposing an 80 to 90 percent tax on any profits accrued that were higher than prewar levels. Importantly, however, it exempted employers' contributions to employee benefits, both health care and pensions. The effect of this special provision was for companies to divert profits into employee benefits in order to avoid the high tax rates. Then, just one year later, the National War Labor Board followed with a decision that such employee fringe benefits should not count as wages. A "no-strike" pledge made by unions during the war prevented them from demanding higher wages, but this new ruling permitted them to channel their efforts toward stronger benefits instead, a goal they could pursue through collective bargaining.[46] Through this haphazard assortment of rulings, public officials inadvertently established for health insurance companies a government-subsidized status, revolving around tax exemption.

Once such policies were in place, they in turn shaped the politics surrounding health care. Health insurance companies, emboldened by the measures they had already won, worked to strengthen and expand their privileged role. Two policies signed into law by President Dwight Eisenhower bolstered their position. Interestingly, by the early 1950s, as the amount of funds involved in health insurance grew and the size of federal subsidies expanded, IRS officials claimed that the tax-exempt status should apply only to conventional insurance—forms other than health insurance. Contradicting that interpretation, Eisenhower advocated for and signed into law the Revenue Act of 1954, which cleared up ambiguities and confirmed the blanket, tax-free status of employer-provided health insurance. The president deliberately promoted it as social policy. Then in 1959 Congress followed with a law granting coverage of federal employees with private insurance.[47] Eisenhower's leadership on both matters continued the tradition of Republicans playing the predominant roles in building the submerged state.

The ascendance of privately provided, government-subsidized health insurance further influenced the goals and activities of labor unions. These organizations found greater leverage in negotiating with employers for private health insurance benefits than in seeking government-sponsored coverage, and it became their chief strategy for recruiting and retaining members. In the mid-twentieth century, they did work hard to achieve both disability coverage under Social Security in 1956 and to establish Medicare for retired workers in 1965, but they offered only lukewarm support at best for policy initiatives for health insurance for all Americans.[48] While the percentage of Americans with private health insurance kept soaring, growing from just 10 percent in 1940 to over 80 percent in 1980, this strategy was not unreasonable.[49] After 1980, however, labor's circumstances changed dramatically, as it diminished in size and increasingly sought to organize and represent workers employed in sectors that lacked established private insurance plans. In the 1993–94 reform cycle, labor organizations still refrained from offering a forceful endorsement of Clinton's reform initiative, although by that time their stance owed partially to their desire for a stronger alternative.[50]

The politics of the submerged state reached a zenith moment during consideration of Clinton's health care plan, complete with powerful interest groups that rallied quickly to oppose it and to defend existing arrangements, and a passive public that lost faith in reform once the battle was under way. Americans received Clinton's plan with warm support when he first introduced it in September 1993, but the interest groups were already energized against it. The Health Insurance Association of America ran the so-called "Harry and Louise" television ads that featured a husband and wife talking at a kitchen table and worrying that "the government may force us to pick from a few health plans designed by government bureaucrats." The Coalition for Health Insurance Choices organized employers in opposition at the grassroots level. It was joined by the National Federation of Independent Business, the Chamber of Commerce, Business Roundtable, and National Association of Manufacturers—all taking part in not only the field operation but also massive lobbying efforts in Washington, D.C., and public relations campaigns nationwide. Republican leaders in Congress, meanwhile, crafted messages to stimulate opposition among the public. Buffeted by all of these forces, public support for reform declined, and by the summer of 1994 it was declared a lost cause.[51]

Interest Groups United for Government Action

Viewed against this daunting history, the ability of the Obama administration and congressional Democrats to work together with organized interests in 2009–10 should be understood as genuine success in creating a broad coalition of support for reform in the public's interest. Officials in the administration gleaned lessons from the legacy of failed health care reform efforts and especially the devastating fate of the Clinton plan. They vowed to avoid mobilizing stakeholder opposition, planning deliberately to bring such groups to the bargaining table and to keep them engaged, hoping to prevent them from turning against plans too early on, if at all.[52] Indeed, such efforts paid off, as organizations that had never before endorsed health care reform came on board in support, and others at least refrained from marshaling their forces against it as soon or as powerfully as in the past.

Health providers, both hospitals and doctors, lent their support to reform. Policymakers assured these parties that reform would benefit them, to the tune of $171 billion and $228 billion, respectively, and they in turn consented to sizable future payment reductions in Medicare.[53] This involved a dramatic, historic reversal on the part of the American Medical Association, which had so long been regarded as an arch foe of government efforts in the health care realm. Because of several modifications it won in the Medicare payment plan, the AMA even endorsed the House plan, complete with the provision of which it disapproved, the so-called "public option" clause. This would have given Americans the right to choose an affordable plan of government-run health coverage, forcing private insurers to compete with it.[54]

The pharmaceutical industry also cooperated in supporting reform—a surprise given that Obama had lambasted it throughout the 2008 campaign. Once elected, he and Senator Baucus worked closely with PhRMA leaders to broker an agreement to reduce the cost of drugs purchased through the Medicare prescription drug benefit and its "doughnut hole" provision that required seniors to pay the full price of some prescriptions. Former congressman Billy Tauzin played a central role for PhRMA, producing a deal that promised the industry billions of dollars from prescriptions for Americans who would be newly insured, as well as additional subsidies through the repair of the "doughnut hole." Tauzin also managed to win guarantees that the drug companies would not have to compete with producers of cheaper generic medications—the direct reversal of a campaign promise by Obama. Although the outcome granted ample rewards to drug companies, nonetheless it simultaneously generated $80 billion in savings to help finance health care reform, brought the AARP on board, and prompted PhRMA to spend millions on advertising in support of the legislation.[55]

The role of private insurance companies, more than that of any other player, epitomizes the politics of the submerged state in health care reform. Initially, America's Health Insurance Plans (AHIP), a trade group of several large insurance companies led by President Karen Ignagni, participated in a White House summit early in 2009 and pledged to reduce costs voluntarily. In May the organization declared itself to be "honored" to "help advance a framework for cost containment" and professed belief that "all Americans must have access to affordable, high-quality health care coverage."[56] Its subsequent action, however, promoted its own interests through a two-pronged approach. On the one hand, AHIP worked against aspects of reform it disliked. It actively opposed the public option proposal and won numerous concessions in the Senate Finance Committee's markup of the bill. It also collected funds from its members—Aetna, Cigna, Humana, and others—to finance television ads disparaging the main proposals being developed in Congress.[57] On the other hand, it strongly supported the "individual mandate" feature that would require all Americans to purchase health insurance. Without this stipulation, adverse selection of unhealthy people into private insurance pools would continue to drive up costs; mandatory insurance would make reform feasible by enlarging risk pools with more young and healthy people, thus lowering costs for all participants. At the same time, the individual mandate promised to deliver millions of new customers into the arms of the private insurers, clearly advantageous for them. In fact, AHIP opposed efforts to weaken the penalties for failure to obtain insurance; they threatened to curtail the number of Americans who would flock to its coverage. As analysts of reform Lawrence R. Jacobs and Theda Skocpol trenchantly observe, it was not the prospect of a "government takeover" of the health care system that most energized the insurance companies. Rather, "too *little* government was what moved insurers into open revolt."[58]

Organized labor, for its part, played a far more active and constructive role in pushing for the adoption of health care reform than in the past. The Service Employees International Union, the AFL-CIO, and the American Federation of State, County, and Municipal Employees all strongly supported the adoption of the public option and thus favored the House plan.[59] Rather than only disparaging the alternatives, unions actively promoted the legislation: they ran ads, their representatives showed up at town meetings to counter the arguments of opponents, and they mobilized in states and districts of swing voters. Organizer Dennis Rivera explained, "We're running this . . . like . . . a presidential campaign, and our candidate is health care reform."[60]

While this degree of cooperation among stakeholders brought reform closer to being realized than ever before, some powerful interests—predominantly business groups—remained opposed. Not all businesses fought reform; some major corporations lent it their support. Still, the Chamber of Commerce and the National Federation of Independent Business mobilized vigorously against proposed changes. The Chamber facilitated the purchase of ads for the insurance companies, and it lobbied persistently, gaining the distinction of the single biggest spender on lobbying during 2009.[61]

Also, as we have already seen, groups that would seem to have little relevance to health care policy—the real estate industry and charitable organizations—mobilized early to oppose the Obama administration's plans for financing reform. Their action to protect the tax policies from which they benefit thwarted the bill's progress at a critical juncture and prompted political leaders to advance instead a tax on high-priced employer-provided health insurance packages. That approach—though possibly one of the most effective tools of cost control—became controversial because it would have affected a number of low- and moderate-income Americans who do have so-called "Cadillac plans" and because unions, whose efforts had helped win such packages, disliked it. The final version of the bill, after changes by the Democratic leadership, deemphasized this financing plan, incorporating only a modest version of it and one not scheduled to begin until 2018, leaving consumers time to shift out of such plans. Instead, the legislation ultimately relied far more heavily on taxes on households with incomes of $250,000 or above.[62] Nonetheless, the obstacles encountered by Obama's original plan had slowed progress on the bill at a critical stage, stymieing forward momentum for reform and further exasperating a weary public.

As this brief summary should make evident, health care reform was anything but a "government takeover" of independent, autonomous market institutions. Rather, reform involved restructuring a set of already existing policies, ones developed long ago through cooperation and negotiation between government and private sector actors—in short, components of the submerged state that nurture the health care sector. Through such arrangements, health insurance companies, hospitals, and drug companies have benefited for decades from government assistance—which they welcomed and sometimes initiated momentum for—in the form of subsidies, favorable regulatory policies, and tax policies. Reformers in 2009 and 2010 sought not to introduce a role for government in health care, but rather to modify the extensive already-existing policies. They aimed to make such policies more efficient by covering more Americans and lowering costs, and they intended to make the terms of coverage fairer and more dependable.

The extent to which interest groups themselves helped facilitate successful reform is remarkable only if we are blind to the existence and historical development of the submerged state. According to the Congressional Budget Office, health insurance will grow from covering 83 percent of the population prior to health care reform to 94 percent once the terms of the Affordable Care Act are implemented. For health insurance companies, this change means 32 million new customers![63] Similarly, the needs of the newly insured and the enhancement of coverage for seniors will mean many more prescriptions for pharmaceutical companies. In short, so-called "private sector" organizations will benefit tremendously from policies that function by channeling the delivery of public policy through them.

Revealing Somewhat More

While the Obama administration succeeded in making clear to interest groups what health care reform meant for them, it spread the word less vigorously among Americans generally. It was not that the president did not speak about the policy in public; to the contrary, in using the bully pulpit during his first fourteen months in office, Obama prioritized health care reform. As figure 4.1 in the previous chapter illustrates, he spoke out on that issue far more frequently than either higher education or tax policy, or even both combined. The complexity of the health care system—involving different sets of arrangements for different people, sometimes

FIGURE 5.2. Obama's Public Statements on Health Care Reform: Revealing the Submerged State, February 2009–March 2010

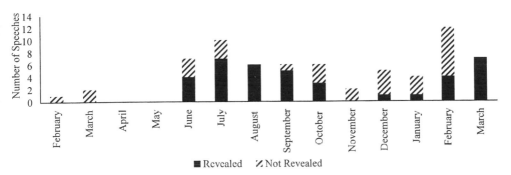

Source: Author's content analysis of "Speeches and Remarks" and "Weekly Addresses" by President Barack Obama, available at White House Briefing Room website, http://www.whitehouse.gov/briefing-room. See text and notes for discussion of coding guidelines.

even within the same household—certainly makes it far more difficult to explain health care policy to the public than other policies, such as student aid reform. Still, Obama did on numerous occasions—thirty-eight out of sixty-eight times—attempt to reveal what was at stake in reconstituting the submerged state in this area.[64]

As figure 5.2 illustrates, Obama waited until the summer of 2009 to start offering frequent speeches about health care reform and to begin exposing the workings of the submerged state in relation to it. This delay likely hindered his efforts, as opponents mobilized more quickly to depict the public option as a "government takeover" and to stoke concerns about new taxes on existing health benefits. By the time the president took to the airwaves, support had already begun to diminish.

Once the president began to make numerous such speeches, he regularly included statements describing how existing arrangements benefited private interests. For example, at an online town hall meeting in July, he said:

> About two-thirds of the costs of the reforms . . . will come from reallocating money that is already being spent in the health care system but isn't being spent wisely. So it doesn't involve more spending; it just involves smarter spending. . . . And I'll just give you one example. . . . Over the next 10 years, we will spend $177 billion . . . in unwarranted subsidies to insurance companies under something called . . . Medicare Advantage. Now, this does not make seniors healthier. People who are signed up for

this private insurance subsidized program don't get any better care than those who aren't. The subsidies don't go to the patients; they go to the insurance companies. Now, think if we took that $177 billion and helped families so that they could have insurance, and that we could have preventive care.[65]

The next month, in Montana, he once again talked about the need to "eliminate subsidies to insurance companies."

I just think I would rather be giving that money to the young lady here who doesn't have health insurance and giving her some help, than giving it to insurance companies that are making record profits.[66]

Obama also tried to explain how Americans with different circumstances—those who had insurance already and those lacking it—would experience the benefits that came with reform. It was an uphill battle: polls revealed that a substantial portion of the population did not grasp key details of the new policy, as they repeatedly expressed faulty assumptions to pollsters, claiming that particular features of the new law were not actually contained within it.

Obama rarely addressed one particular aspect of health care reform that greatly concerned many Americans: the expected cost of the changes and who would pay for them. Of course, the administration largely left financing decisions to Congress, as we have seen, and there they remained in flux nearly until the very final votes on passage in March 2010. Meanwhile, however, the public likely found little clarity and assurance on questions that provoked worry. Without making these dimensions of the submerged state visible to the public, Obama may have left Americans more easily swayed by the arguments of opponents, who repeatedly equated health care reform with higher taxes.

As the months passed, polls showed that many Americans became less supportive of the reform proposal overall. Public opinion analyst Robert Blendon found that, similar to patterns in the 1993–94 reform cycle, by late in 2009 the majority of Americans did not feel that a new law would help them or their families personally, but rather that it would have adverse consequences, increasing their taxes or diminishing the quality of their care.[67] These opinions cannot be explained simply as emanating from some enduring sense of "American values," such as individualism and limited government. Indeed, polls had long found widespread support for health care reform.[68] Furthermore, large majorities of Americans continued to express support for specific policy elements included in the final bill, such as requiring insurers to cover those with existing conditions and coverage of adult children up through age twenty-six.[69] The attributes of the submerged state help to explain these anomalies, highlighting why the prospect of what opponents termed a "government takeover" could be unsettling to people who already have employer-provided insurance or even a more visible policy like Medicare, with some submerged features. First, they may not perceive government's already extensive role in their health care policy, so the prospect of government intervention would likely appear to be a new and foreign idea. Second, they may not grasp how proposed reforms—such as measures to increase the size of risk pools and new regulations on insurance companies—could possibly help to improve circumstances for their own families, given that the new policies are also to operate through the hidden pathways of the submerged state.

In addition, while many citizens may have received insufficient information about how reform would affect them, what they could observe clearly in media coverage was the numerous special deals that lawmakers made in the process of arriving at a bill. Repeatedly, congressional leaders and the president negotiated with stakeholder interest groups and with a handful of individual lawmakers whose votes were deemed crucial. Each of these interactions resulted in the negotiation of privileged treatment for particular interests, whether Nebraskans, union members, or drug companies. While such agreements helped move the policy closer to passage, they likely appeared to citizens as excessive catering to special interests. Such politics likely strike many—particularly independents, who have less knowledge of the political process generally—as undemocratic, and at odds with the open and accessible forms of governance Obama had promised during his campaign.

Nonetheless, although public doubts and opposition to reform grew, support remained stronger than had been the case during the Clinton effort in 1993–94. On the eve of the bill's final passage in March 2010, 46 percent said they favored the proposals being considered in Congress compared to 42 percent who said they opposed them.[70] Certainly these poll results fail to compare to the impressive support enjoyed by major policies such as Medicare soon after its passage, but that not only occurred in a period without the strong political polarization of the present; it also involved the creation of a visible policy, not the overhaul of an established part of the submerged state. Health policy scholar Mark Schlesinger has suggested that the fact that in 2010 a larger portion of the public continued to support reform than to oppose it, which had not occurred in 1994, emboldened policymakers as they took the final step to vote for passage.[71] Though Obama's efforts at revealing the submerged state to the public could have started earlier and been more pointed and sustained, nonetheless they may have helped to move the legislative package across the finish line.

Modifying and Expanding the Submerged State

Time and again, reformers' hopes have been dashed in the pursuit of health care reform, and yet this time, despite the obstacles, they prevailed. After ninety years of effort, the achievement is momentous. It promises to expand health care coverage to 32 million young and working-age Americans and, by imposing new regulations on insurance companies, to grant people greater security that they will not be denied coverage, for example, if they become sick. In some significant ways, the policy expands the visible state, particularly by making more Americans eligible for Medicaid. In other ways, it enlarges the submerged state, channeling more people toward private insurance and offering them tax breaks to help pay for it.

The Obama administration succeeded at reform because officials were willing to negotiate with vested interests, finding ways to gain their cooperation. But when policy achievements are won through the submerged state, even a major victory—one that years' worth of polling suggested Americans wanted—does not guarantee strong public support. In recognition of this, after signing the historic legislation, Obama toured the country making speeches to explain to Americans what the new policy entailed and what it would mean for their lives. Of course, opponents continued to press their case as well, particularly leading up to the midterm elections. While today's highly polarized political environment itself heightens the difficulties involved in securing public approval for any new law, policymaking involving the submerged state greatly exacerbates such challenges.

Going forward, the public's view will be influenced not only by political discourse, but also by the implementation process—how it is carried out and by how it is experienced personally by individual citizens. Administrators will have the opportunity to shape delivery so that the submerged state undergirding health care provision is made more visible. Reformers included in the law plans for a delivery feature to facilitate this: henceforth, W-2 forms will list the cost of health insurance paid for by employers.[72] It remains to be seen whether this information will be presented in a manner that makes evident government's subsidy for the benefits, embodied in their tax-free status. Through this and myriad other choices about the details of policy delivery, public officials will have the opportunity to help citizens understand government's role in providing for their health care.

In both taxes and health care reform, the Obama administration met with a powerful submerged state, armed and ready to protect the status quo. In its efforts to scale back tax expenditures that benefit the wealthy and powerful interests, it encountered overwhelming resistance, as even members of the president's own party defended existing arrangements. Meanwhile, the president himself acted to greatly enlarge the submerged state through ample new tax expenditures in the stimulus bill. In health care policy, the administration managed to do what no other administration has done, bringing vested interests on board and keeping them together in support of coverage for working-age Americans. The complex new policy, however, is designed to operate as much through the submerged state as through its visible counterparts. As profound an accomplishment as it is in historical perspective, health care reform will do little to repair the relationship between citizens and government unless policy delivery and implementation, going forward, reveal to Americans more clearly the operation of the government.

6 · TOWARD VISIBLE AND VIBRANT DEMOCRACY

For Mary and Joe Thompson of Overland Park, Kansas, September 23, 2010, marked a banner day. In 1999 they had adopted a daughter, Emily, who came to them with spina bifida. Soon after, their residential remodeling business failed, and they sought other employment, which meant acquiring new health insurance. The problem was that insurers refused to cover Emily, who was deemed to have a "preexisting condition." Neither would they cover an older brother in the family, who has attention deficit disorder. But now, six months after Obama signed the health care reform law, one of the its first components went into effect: a rule forbidding insurance companies from denying coverage to children with preexisting medical problems. Said Mary Thompson, "It really is a pinch-me moment. Could it possibly be, after all these years of fighting and jumping through hoops and trying to find the right place to help us out, that she could just be put on our policy with her sister and not be discriminated against any more?"[1]

For some Americans, like the Thompsons, the effects of the Patient Protection and Affordable Care Act were immediately visible and profound, while for others, they were less than clear, put off for the future and buried in submerged policies. The impact was likely evident enough for people such as young adults, many of whom were struggling to find jobs in the weak economy, who could now stay on their parents' insurance up to age twenty-six; and for individuals with a severe medical condition, who could no longer be refused insurance because of lifetime caps on coverage. Many Americans remained doubtful, however, that health care reform would be helpful to their own families, and 45 percent continued to say they were confused about what reform entailed—down from 55 percent in April, but still a large portion of the public.[2] Owing to such reactions, in the same week that the Thompsons greeted reform with appreciation, 61 percent of likely voters told pollsters they favored its repeal.[3]

When the midterm elections came around, rather than rewarding Obama and the congressional Democrats for achieving what political leaders had tried unsuccessfully to accomplish for the better part of a century, instead voters gave them what the president himself termed a "shellacking."[4] Earlier presidents who signed major social legislation into law had not encountered the same treatment. In the presidential election of 1936, held the year after he signed the Social Security Act, Roosevelt himself won by a larger margin than in the previous election, and the Democrats picked up twelve seats. Of course, any president is more likely to see losses for his party in a midterm election; that is what Lyndon Johnson faced, for example, one year after signing Medicare into law. But whereas the Democrats lost forty-seven seats in 1966, they relinquished sixty-three to the Republicans in 2010.

Granted, political circumstances are different today than they were in earlier eras of reform, not least because the middle of the twentieth century was characterized by considerably less political polarization. Numerous moderate Republicans served in Congress, and they often joined together with Democrats in support of social legislation. Over recent decades, such individuals have disappeared, and the differences in the issue positions of the average Democrat and the average Republican member have grown more distinct. The Republican Party in Congress has become more unified and more consistently conservative.[5] Not a single Republican voted in favor of health care reform, and none or almost none supported other major initiatives of the Obama administration. As a result, party leaders made the wager that they had nothing to lose politically and everything to gain by continuing—even after the bill's enactment—to criticize it sharply, thus stoking the calls for repeal. Once they took back the majority in the House in January 2011, Speaker John Boehner immediately called for a vote to repeal health care reform, and it passed by an overwhelming 245 to 189, with three Democrats joining all Republicans to vote in favor of it.

The contemporary media also makes it more difficult than in the past for presidents to rally support for their initiatives. When President Franklin D. Roosevelt gave his "Fireside Chats," he faced little competition on the airwaves. A large portion of American households, typically two-thirds to three-quarters of all, would turn on their radios and tune in to those speeches.[6] By contrast, Obama's State of the Union addresses were watched in only 33 percent of households in 2009, 30 percent in 2010, and 27 percent in 2011.[7] Today, with the proliferation of cable television channels and Internet sources of news, political leaders lack the same ability to dominate the media. Moderates are more likely to tune out entirely, leaving politics to those with stronger ideological leanings, who are less likely to be swayed by new information.[8] In addition, many Americans pay attention increasingly to single sources of biased partisan coverage that reinforces their own views without presenting alternative approaches.

The rise of political polarization and the more fragmented and partisan media notwithstanding, we cannot explain the challenges of contemporary politics without understanding the existence of the submerged state and the dynamics it engenders. For many Americans, the significance of the major pieces of legislation Obama signed in 2009 and 2010—providing economic security and opportunity to ordinary Americans—was simply not clear and apparent. This emanates from the fact that his reform efforts required the reconstitution of submerged policies, those situated in the tax system or taking the form of subsidies and favorable regulations for private organizations. The political process through which such legislation was enacted, moreover, showcased the influence of interest groups, providing yet further evidence to many citizens that the political system was not for and about people like them. As the case studies have demonstrated, reform of the submerged state is extremely difficult and often impossible, and yet even if one overcomes the multiple obstacles and succeeds, as Obama did in many ways, still the public is unlikely to recognize the achievement or to reward reformers.

The submerged state need not, however, remain obscured from view. Opportunities exist to expose it: first, throughout the legislative process, as reformers attempt to overhaul existing policies and to create new ones; and second, later on, in the course of policy delivery. Policymakers can seize moments of policy enactment to transform the submerged state in several ways: to *reconfigure* the role of vested interests that benefit from it; to *reveal* what is at stake to the public through political communication; and to *redesign* policies to make them more visible. After policies are enacted, public officials and organizations can also reveal the submerged state to citizens through policy delivery and communication that make its operations clearer and more transparent. This chapter will compare and assess the degree of success that the Obama administration achieved in these regards through the policymaking efforts examined in this book. It will also offer specific suggestions for how, going forward, governance can be made more obvious to Americans, enabling them to be more engaged as citizens.

The Curious Incident

In his first two years in office, Obama set out to transform social welfare policies ensconced within the submerged state. He sought to scale back or terminate some components that channel funds toward the affluent and vested interests, and to use the savings to create or expand policies that could better meet the needs of low- and moderate-income Americans. He also planned to retain or enlarge other aspects, but to restructure them to distribute benefits more fairly, to mitigate inequality. This constituted a daunting reform agenda.

Notably, Obama's goals did not extend to revealing the submerged state and making governance more visible: reform focused, rather, on changing the material costs and benefits of public policies. This approach is entirely in keeping with the prevailing model of policy analysis, which seeks alternatives offering the greatest efficiency, allowing firms and consumers to maximize utility. The problem with this approach is that it overlooks entirely the political context in which public policies are created and implemented. Such myopia hinders efforts to promote and pass legislation and, for those laws that do become enacted, it imperils the prospects for their sustainability. Moreover, in Obama's case it thwarts his broader goals of reconnecting citizens with government. A reform initiative enacted without attention to revealing the submerged state is analogous to the tree that falls in the forest when no one is around: the event goes unheard, its impact unperceived. To invoke another metaphor, reform involving the submerged state is akin to Sherlock Holmes's "curious incident of the dog in the nighttime": just as the dog's failure to bark while the murder occurred owed to the presence of a particular individual, namely, its owner,[9] the public's failure to notice the significance of reform was attributable to the presence of the submerged state.

The question is, can reform be considered successful if it goes unnoticed? In a system of representative government, the answer is no. A new law may reduce economic inequality by transferring resources to low- and middle-income people, but if it neglects to reveal to citizens what government will do or has done on their behalf, it may likely fail. It may not garner sufficient support from citizens to strengthen the resolve of enough elected officials to vote in favor of it, ensuring its passage. If enacted, if may prove unsustainable, as opponents dismantle it or undermine implementation. It may leave many of its proponents vulnerable at the next election, and if they lose their seats, it will be abandoned by its best defenders and may prove unsustainable. And it will surely mean that the policy does nothing to restore citizens' confidence in government, their awareness of the role government plays in their lives, or their engagement in the political process. In short, what might appear to be a momentous achievement may easily disintegrate.

A Rubric for Reform

Viewed in these terms, how can we assess the extent to which Obama succeeded in revealing the submerged state to citizens? Here I will offer a rubric, a scoring tool that outlines key criteria that can be used in making such evaluations, shown in table 6.1. I will then apply this rubric to the Obama administration, evaluating its record across the three cases considered in this book. It should be noted that the essential condition for reform of the submerged state is that its policies are made more equitable, distributed more broadly in a manner that helps average citizens. But while policy change does not qualify as reform without lessening inequality, my main point is that reform cannot succeed unless the submerged state is revealed in the process. The rubric therefore focuses on the extent of its exposure.

First, policymakers must *reconfigure the role of vested interests* that have benefited from existing arrangements. Ideally, such interests would be defeated entirely, which would create the best prospects for genuine reform. The political circumstances for this rarely occur, however, given that interest groups have managed to build a base of political support over many decades and have ample resources at their disposal to fight reform. Typically, instead, reformers must find ingenious ways to gain interest groups' support while still managing to curtail their power in critical respects. If interest group power remains entirely intact, policy change may still occur, but it would not constitute reform of the submerged state in any meaningful fashion.

Obama's reform efforts during 2009 and 2010 generated all three variants of outcomes in terms of reconfiguring the role of vested interests. In higher education policy, the student lenders met with outright defeat. This was possible because they had already been substantially weakened over time, as journalists and political actors revealed their inappropriate relationships with financial aid officers on campuses, and ultimately through their demise once the credit crisis of 2008 hit. Meanwhile, the direct lending program created in 1993, though for years maintaining only a precarious foothold, had emerged as a feasible alternative means of lending to students without subsidizing banks as middlemen. By contrast, in health care policy, the administration adopted the strategy of working together with key interests to marshal their support for reform. Given how deeply entrenched and powerful such organizations had become, it is difficult to imagine reform succeeding otherwise in 2009–10; as recently as 1993–94, policymakers failed to enlist interest groups' cooperation, and reform unraveled as a result. By necessity, however, this approach

TABLE 6.1. Rubric for Assessment: Extent to Which Reforms Reveal the Submerged State

Criteria	Technique	Performance Rating		
		High: Reveals Governance	Moderate: Continues Submerged State but Constrains or Curtails Scope	Low: Perpetuates or Expands Submerged State
During Legislative Process	Reconfigure Role of Vested Interests	Defeat interest groups entirely (student lending)	Negotiate with groups and gain their support for reform (health care reform)	Groups' position left entirely intact (tax expenditures)
	Reveal through Political Communication	Frequent, sustained attention; high-profile events and venues; makes submerged features clear	Moderate level of effort to reveal clearly and consistently to the public (health care reform)	Little attempt to reveal to public; statements infrequent and/or reveal little (student loans, tax expenditures)
	Reveal through Policy Design	Make government's role explicit through direct visible policies (direct lending; expansion of Medicaid)	Make policies of submerged state more subject to government regulation and limits (role of private insurance companies; health care reform)	Perpetuates or expands size and scope of submerged state (creation of new tax expenditures in stimulus bill)
After Policy Enactment	Reveal through Policy Delivery	Use statements and procedures that make government's role clear (potential for all new policies, but not yet planned)	Use statements and procedures that make apparent the role of private actors but not of government (likely outcome of W-2 information and direct lending)	No procedures or statements adopted
	Reveal through State, Local, or Organizational Efforts	Using campaigns, newsletters, magazines, and websites, make policy operations/effects apparent; frequently, clearly	Using campaigns, newsletters, magazines, and websites, make policy operations/effects apparent; occasionally, less clearly	No such efforts

of involving the interest groups perpetuated the submerged state rather than eradicating it; the embrace of a completely different alternative, such as a single-payer system, appeared to be completely infeasible. Finally, the area of tax expenditures illustrates how formidable the interest groups that benefit from the submerged state can be: they mobilized quickly and closed all discussion of reform; in fact, given the immense leverage they enjoy with policymakers, this outcome appeared to have been a foregone conclusion.

Second, reformers must *reveal to the public what is at stake in reform through political communication.* They must expose existing policies of the submerged state, making it clear how they operate and who benefits from them. They must also explain clearly how new policies would function, who will gain, and what the costs will be. The extent of revealing depends on the frequency of public statements about the topic, how much those statements actually reveal about what is at stake in reform, the timing of such statements, and whether or not such messages are conveyed in highly visible venues or occasions.

While Obama has done more than other political leaders to date to expose the deeply obscured arrangements of the submerged state, still more sustained and focused attention on these matters would have better enabled citizens to understand what reform entailed and the value it held for their own lives. Given the centrality of restructuring the submerged state to his reform agenda, it was particularly important for him to place emphasis on it in his public addresses. Earlier and more deliberate communication by the president might have helped to keep the public more engaged in and supportive of reform. Ironically, the president revealed the submerged state most fully and eloquently when he spoke about student loan reform—but he barely ever did. Conversely, he spoke about taxes in general quite often but almost never about tax expenditures and how they operate. The president's communication about health care reform deserves the highest grade of the three for both the frequency and deliberateness of his statements, but even then such efforts were delayed and did far less than they could have to maintain public engagement in the process. Still, his efforts on health care may have helped keep public opinion supportive enough to bolster the resolve of some critical swing voters in Congress who voted in favor of reform on final passage.

Targeted statements on specific policies can be a start to revealing the submerged state, but in isolated form they are hardly enough. The broader message of this book is that we need to have a new, honest, and sustained conversation about how governance operates in the United States. As long as public officials criticize government but persist in channeling public resources surreptitiously through private means, Americans will be deluded. They will ascribe more autonomy to the market than it is due, and less legitimacy to government than it deserves. Visionary leaders need to commence that discussion, one that is essential not only given the nation's current social and economic problems and fiscal plight, but also for the sake of democratic renewal.

Nor are political discourse and communication the only means, nor necessarily the best means, through which to convey information about policies to the public. More effective and enduring approaches operate through mechanisms that people experience on a personal basis. These include features of policy design, aspects of policy delivery, and publicity provided by organizations and state and local leaders. Most prominent among these is policy design, a critical yet often overlooked aspect of the policy process.

Namely, third, reformers must *redesign policies to make governance more visible to citizens*. Policy design refers to the particular rules, procedures, administrative arrangements, and financing mechanisms inscribed in laws. As we saw in chapter 2, social benefits are most clearly visible to citizens when they are set up to be administered directly by government rather than channeled through the tax system, run through benefits from private employers, or managed by subsidized private actors. Policymakers can best enable citizens to understand how governance works—both during reform and especially thereafter—if such arrangements are adapted. If no political support exists for this, reformers may choose to continue overall existing policies of the submerged state or to create new ones, but to do so in a manner that at least curtails the degree of support for private actors and regulates it more effectively than in the past. If neither of these approaches is used, whatever new policies are adopted will fall short of reform, only strengthening and expanding the submerged state.

Much of contemporary reform efforts will take the middle path, harnessing the submerged state more effectively for public purposes, so it is worth noting how even within that approach, variation in policy design can influence how visible policies become. For instance, tax expenditures are not all uniformly hidden; some have features that help make them somewhat more visible. The Earned Income Tax Credit, for example, is more evident to individuals as a social benefit than is the Home Mortgage Interest Deduction. These differences emanate in part from the fact that the EITC, being a refundable tax credit, is received by the vast majority of claimants as a lump sum payment—a check received in the mail—following their filing of tax forms.[10] The HMID, by contrast, functions to reduce claimant's taxable income at amounts that vary with their tax rate and the amount they paid in mortgage interest. Taxpayers who itemize their deductions—only 36 percent of all—file for the HMID on the same form on which they may note the value of their charitable contributions, state and local property taxes, and other factors.[11] They are unlikely to acquire any sense of how much they gained from any one of these tax breaks in particular.

In policy design, the Obama administration's efforts produced a full range of outcomes with respect to visibility. In student aid policy, the transformation from bank-based to direct lending goes further than any other change to make government's role more obvious. The new arrangements will make citizens' needs primary, rather than prioritizing the interest of lenders to make profits. The question remains, however, whether citizens will grasp this difference given that, remarkably, banks will retain authority for servicing of loans.

The health care bill encompassed a wide variety of approaches to policy design, and Americans will thus perceive the role of government to varying extents depending on which aspect of the health care system most influences their lives. In some respects, the new law enlarges visible governance, most notably by making more Americans eligible for Medicaid. In the main, however, it perpetuates the submerged state, channeling millions of new customers toward insurance companies for coverage. At the same time, it does offer new regulations to constrain the activities of such companies, for example, by forbidding them to eliminate people with preexisting conditions from coverage, requiring them to cover children through age twenty-six on their parents' insurance, and so forth. The projected tax on the most expensive health care plans as of 2018 will also reduce the scope of subsidies for employer-provided health insurance to some extent.

In tax policy, the Obama administration has greatly expanded the submerged state. Aside from the above-mentioned limits on "Cadillac plans," none of the president's proposals for scaling back the generosity of tax expenditures for the wealthiest Americans have gained political traction. Yet Obama found it remarkably easy to include in the stimulus the new tax expenditures that he had promised during the campaign, including Making Work Pay and the American Opportunity Tax Credit, as well as numerous others. This record illustrates that in the contemporary polity, no policy initiatives can be enacted more easily than new or expanded tax breaks. However, such policies are antithetical to effective reform, as they sharply reduce federal revenues and citizens barely notice them, even when they gain from them themselves. In fact, they fail to influence even citizens' views about the tax system, not to mention their perception that government assists them or provides opportunities for them. Whatever the social and economic effects of such tax expenditures might be—and the record is not promising even on those scores—they are counterproductive when it comes to reinvigorating citizenship.

After Policy Enactment

Though journalists, pundits, and political scientists tend to focus especially on what happens when issues are on the policy agenda and being actively debated by Congress, crucial experiences in shaping citizens' understanding of government also occur quite apart from those moments. They take place as citizens themselves seek to qualify for or claim social benefits, as they become aware of their friends and family members' experiences in doing so, or as they hear about them—or fail to do so—through the media or other sources aside from political actors at the federal level. This means that in order to think about whether the submerged state is becoming more or less visible to Americans, we need to also look past policy reform to the events that follow. As noted eloquently by political scientist Eric Patashnik, "The second phase of reform begins the moment *after* the curtain falls on the high drama of legislative enactments."[12]

Meaningful information about how policies work can be provided to individuals through *policy delivery*. Though policy design establishes the structure and form of policies, variation in how particular features are made manifest to citizens can be influenced through the procedures administrators use, both in making benefits available and in informing the public about them. This is exemplified by what amounted to a natural experiment conducted by the Social Security Administration some years ago, when it first began to send an annual personal statement to some individuals—but not yet to all—about the value of the benefits they and their family members would receive if and when they became disabled or retired. Political scientists Fay Lomax Cook, Lawrence R. Jacobs, and Dukhong Kim examined how the receipt of such information influenced recipients' understanding and attitudes. Controlling for individual characteristics, they found that it elevated recipients' knowledge of and confidence in the program. They conclude, "Decisions by government officials about the amount, kind, and delivery vehicle for the distribution of information may have a measurable impact on public knowledge and confidence in government."[13]

It is not clear that policymakers in 2009 and 2010 did much to consider how the processes of policy delivery might affect citizens' perceptions. On the one hand, future W-2 forms will contain information about employer-provided health insurance benefits, and, depending on how the information is presented, it may help make people more aware that these benefits are tax-free. On the other hand, policy officials seem inattentive to how the one program they managed to excavate fully from the submerged state—student loans—could be delivered in such a way as to make government's role more apparent.

Just as behavioral economists have experimented with the features of forms to see which facilitate enrollment in retirement savings programs or in college, we need to explore how specific types of statements and reports for beneficiaries of social policies affect their understanding of government's role in providing their benefits and of their value and effects. In the case of student loans, for example, applicants and borrowers could receive information presented in a manner similar to how retirement investors such as TIAA-CREF inform people about different investment scenarios. Just as they typically portray the investment approaches of a hypothetical "John" and "Mary" and compare their projected returns, a simple flyer or webpage tool could indicate the costs over time of a given amount if it is borrowed through a direct loan (or FFEL, for borrowers from the past), with low costs facilitated by government, compared to a private loan unsubsidized by government. For health care policy, Americans could receive an annual statement comparable to those used by the Social Security Administration, explaining the extent to which government either lowers the cost of their employer-provided insurance or pays for their coverage directly. For the next several years, such statements could also indicate the relevant provisions of the Patient Protection and Affordable Care Act of 2010 that affect individual households, such as changes in prescription drug coverage for seniors, coverage of young adults in families with children, and so forth. In order to reveal more about tax expenditures, the Internal Revenue Service could provide households with a statement after the payment of taxes that indicates how much was accrued through each claimed benefit. It could also indicate the amount families would owe if employer benefits for health care and retirement were taxed, thus making apparent the savings that households enjoy.

Much can also be communicated to citizens about public benefits through *campaigns by state and local governments*, encouraging their residents to claim federal benefits for which they are eligible. For example, some states and localities have helped make the EITC more visible to their citizens in order to expand the number of claims, thus helping to bring money into their communities and stimulating the local economy. In many areas, public officials have organized efforts to publicize the availability of program benefits and to provide free assistance to individuals in completing the necessary paperwork to qualify for it.[14] Other such benefits of the submerged state could also be revealed to citizens through comparable efforts.

Similarly, *civic associations and other organizations* can play a role in making Americans aware of benefits within the submerged state.[15] Organizations often played this role historically, as in the case of veterans' associations spreading information about the G.I. Bill. In 2009–10, as reform efforts were being considered in Congress, some groups made information available to their members through their websites, newsletters, and magazines. Labor unions and the American Association of Retired Persons notified their members about health care proposals and what their specific features would mean for them. Similarly, the United States Student Association and Public Interest Research Group, both the national group and its state affiliates, provided their members with legislative updates about student aid proposals. As implementation of new policies proceeds, such organizations provide an excellent conduit for explaining to members how benefits work and what value they have.

Seemingly Stateless Political Development

Since the 1970s, the United States has experienced soaring economic inequality, stagnating rates of educational attainment, and health insecurity on the rise. The problem is not that American policymakers have done nothing—as a percentage of GDP, U.S. government obligations to social welfare have kept pace with those of comparable nations.[16] What is distinct in the United States is the extent to which those commitments are channeled through the submerged state, rather than through visible governance, and in a manner that is upwardly redistributive.

Paradoxically, the penchant for smaller government in the United States, particularly over the past thirty years of conservative dominance, has given us governance as costly as it is elsewhere, but that is uniquely invisible. At the same time, while market forces have stalled income growth among most Americans while increasing the riches of the most affluent, the submerged state—rather than mitigating economic inequality—has sharply exacerbated its effects. Also, these hidden policies, by nurturing governance that cannot be seen by most people while it is plainly evident to those who reap the largest gains, have promoted political inequality. Most people are unaware of the upward bias of these policies or that they even exist; even beneficiaries themselves are often incognizant, and, unaware that it is government that aids them, they embrace anti-government attitudes. Stateless governance does not beget citizens; rather, it breeds cynicism and alienation.

The high cost and perverse effects of the submerged state are not unknown to most policy experts. Economists have criticized its policies for years.[17] Bipartisan presidential commissions, including those named by Ronald Reagan and George W. Bush, have called for termination or sharp reduction of the Home Mortgage Interest Deduction and many other tax breaks. In each instance, such recommendations have quickly met with resounding opposition, and the reports have been ignored. Most recently, these events repeated themselves when a commission named by Obama, chaired by former Republican senator Alan Simpson and Bill Clinton's chief of staff, Erskine Bowles, suggested transforming the HMID into a 12 percent nonrefundable tax credit for all, limited to first mortgages only and capped at those worth $500,000. As soon as such reports were publicized, the realtors' lobby protested loudly, claiming the change would be devastating for the housing market and the economy, and members of both parties on Capitol Hill spoke out to agree.[18] The commission report subsequently failed to garner the necessary fourteen out of eighteen votes required for it to be sent to Congress for consideration. In a déjà vu of events during 2009, a plan that could have mitigated inequality and made good fiscal sense was decimated by the powerful interests that protect the submerged state.

As the 111th Congress came to a close, it complied with Obama's request to support a bill that renewed the Bush tax cuts for all—including the affluent—for two more years, while also extending unemployment insurance benefits. Commentators focused on the fact that while the president had long wished to allow the reductions for the wealthiest American to expire, the still-sluggish economy and the midterm election results prompted him to agree to the compromise with Republicans. Two more subtle points, both involving the ironies of politics conducted through the submerged state, failed to receive attention. First, because of the phased-in effects of the Bush tax cuts, the rollback of the 1990 limits on tax breaks for the rich only reached their full effect in 2010, and now Obama—who had previously sought to reinstate such limits—was in fact extending the most generous treatment of the most privileged Americans. Second, the administration also scaled back the payroll tax from 6.2 to 4.2 percent, a provision that polls found most Americans disliked because they feared it would weaken the Social Security system. While such a policy is enormously expensive—estimated at $111.7 billion over ten years—it is highly likely that just like the tax cuts in the stimulus bill, its benefits will elude most Americans.[19] The bill may produce the desired effect of stimulating the economy, but it is unlikely to make citizens more aware of how government makes a difference in their lives.

Reinvigorating Democracy

In a democracy, the most basic task of governance—more fundamental than stimulating the economy, providing health care and education, or protecting the environment—is to promote the conditions that make rule by the people possible. For citizens to possess the political power to rule themselves, they need to understand their own relationship to government and the role it does and does not play in their lives. As early as the nineteenth century, American public officials chose to direct public funds through private channels, and that pattern has become increasingly common in our own time, as illustrated by the social policies examined in this book. Yet such arrangements leave citizens oblivious to how much government itself is responsible for the vibrancy of whole sectors of the market and for protecting Americans' well-being. The politics that ensues—dominated by sophisticated and powerful stakeholders but absent citizens—is anything but democratic. Such dynamics exacerbate economic inequality, intensify and elevate the role of interest groups, and undermine active and informed citizenship. As a result, the submerged state imperils efforts to direct government's purpose to the common good.

When Obama first declared his candidacy and then as he assumed the highest office in the land, he promised that his presidency would help Americans to "reclaim the meaning of citizenship," "restore our sense of common purpose," and "restore the vital trust between people and their government." Reconstituting the submerged state may appear distant from or antithetical to such goals, but in fact it is crucial. If conducted successfully, it can diffuse the power of special interests relative to that of the public and channel resources to ordinary Americans, thus mitigating inequality. If citizens are simultaneously reengaged through political communication, policy design, and policy delivery, reform can help to reinvigorate American democracy.

APPENDIX

Text and Graphics for Additional Experimental
Questions and Treatments

Retirement Savings Contribution Tax Credit

Do you favor or oppose the Retirement Savings Contribution Tax Credit?

a. Favor strongly
b. Favor somewhat
c. Oppose somewhat
d. Oppose strongly
e. Don't know/no opinion

Group One Treatment: Here is some information about the federal Retirement Savings Contribution Tax Credit. This policy is a tax benefit for people who invest in private retirement plans administered by their employers. These plans include stocks, bonds, and real estate. Under this policy, people do not have to pay taxes on income they use for these investments.

Group Two Treatment: [Same statement as Group One, plus the following language and fig. A.1:] The people who benefit most from this policy are those who have the highest incomes. In 2000 a majority of the benefits went to people who lived in households that made $75,000 or more that year.

Earned Income Tax Credit

Do you favor or oppose the federal Earned Income Tax Credit?

a. Favor strongly
b. Favor somewhat
c. Oppose somewhat

FIGURE A.1. Who Benefits from the Retirement Savings Contribution Tax Credit?

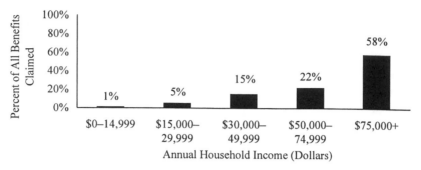

Source: Congressional Budget Office, "Utilization of Tax Incentives for Retirement Savings: An Update" (February 2006), http://www.cbo.gov/ftpdocs/70xx/doc7043/02-10-TaxIncentives.pdf.

FIGURE A.2. Who Benefits from the Earned Income Tax Credit?

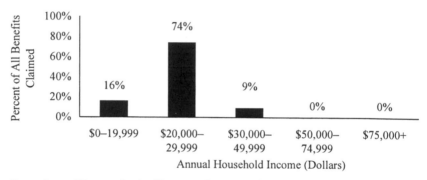

Source: Internal Revenue Service, "Statistics of Income: Individual Complete Report 2004," Publication 1304, table 3.3., http://www.irs.gov/taxstats/indtaxstats/article/0,,id=134951,00.html.

d. Oppose strongly

e. Don't know/no opinion

Group One Treatment: Here is some information about the federal Earned Income Tax Credit. This is a tax benefit for people who work but do not make much money. Under this policy, many people pay no taxes on their income, and some actually receive a payment from the government if their income is low enough.

Group Two Treatment: [Same as Group One, plus the following language and fig. A.2:] The people who benefit most from this policy are those who have low incomes. In 2004 a large majority of the benefits went to people who lived in households that made less than $30,000 that year.

ACKNOWLEDGMENTS

In retrospect, this book's development bears a striking parallel to the submerged state: I was working on it for several years before I became aware of it and realized what I was doing. In fact, while focused on other book projects, I might never have become cognizant of its stealth emergence among them had it not been pointed out to me by three very astute people. The first to notice was my own dear daughter Sophie. A college student studying politics herself and a political activist, she listened to me describe the argument in a conference paper I was writing and said, "Mom, you should write a book about this!" Next my good friend Madonna Harrington-Meyer, a savvy sociologist with keen judgment, responded in kind. Completing this convincing triumvirate, Larry Jacobs offered sage advice about the shape such a book could take, and pointed me toward the book series he co-edits at the University of Chicago Press. I am thankful to each of these individuals for their foresight and encouragement.

I would not have taken the plunge into experimental research had it not been for Matt Guardino, a PhD student at Syracuse University who became my partner in learning about experiments and then in designing and carrying out the research and analysis that underscores chapter 3 of this book. I have learned so much from Matt, and this book would not be the same without his influence on my thinking.

Several research assistants at Cornell University helped make this book possible. Julianna Koch has proven truly indispensable, given her own in-depth knowledge of tax expenditures and her remarkable ability, tenacity, and care in conducting research. Danielle Thomsen, Deondra Rose, and Alexis Walker each also took time away from their own fascinating projects and provided excellent help in bringing this book to fruition.

I have been fortunate to know many wonderful colleagues who have each contributed to this book in some crucial way. My thinking about hidden aspects of governance has long been influenced by the pathbreaking scholarship of Jacob Hacker and Christopher Howard. Danny Hayes generously served as a guiding light as I took my first foray into experimental research; I am ever grateful for his extensive feedback at each stage in the process. Matt Cleary and Peter Enns also helped me to think these matters through. A generous invitation from Desmond King and Larry Jacobs to write a paper for a conference they hosted at Oxford University provided the critical impetus that drove me to formulate the ideas presented here. At the conference, I received useful comments from both of them as well as from E. J. Dionne, Kimberly Johnson, Adam Sheingate, and Helen Thompson. Two astute anonymous reviewers for the University of Chicago Press read the entire book manuscript and provided extensive and invaluable advice for which I am most appreciative.

Organizations and institutions helped make the research possible. The Social and Governmental Issues and Participation Survey of 2008, analyzed in the second half of chapter 2, was funded by grants from the Russell Sage Foundation and the Spencer Foundation. Joanne Miller offered smart suggestions on survey design, and the Survey Research Institute at Cornell University conducted the survey. The experiment underlying chapter 3 was made possible by Time-Sharing Experiments in the Social Sciences (TESS), which fielded the questions. Diana Mutz and others at TESS gave helpful advice on the experiment's design. The Spencer Foundation also funded the research that made chapter 4 possible, and I am especially appreciative of the individuals in Washington, D.C., who kindly permitted me to interview them on the politics of higher education policy. A study leave from Cornell University enabled me to complete the writing process.

At the University of Chicago Press, my editor John Tryneski has gone above and beyond the call of duty, offering incisive suggestions at each stage of the process. I am also thankful to Erin DeWitt, Micah Fehrenbacher, Rodney Powell, and all of the others at the Press who helped to usher the book through the production process. Portions of this book appeared in very different form in an article published earlier: "Reconstituting the Submerged State: The Challenges of Social Policy Reform in the Obama Era," *Perspectives on Politics* 8 (2010): 803–24.

As always, my family has made it all possible, providing steadfast encouragement and making every day a joy. Long conversations with Wayne Grove, the sustenance of my life, once again helped me to think about things in new ways and to solve myriad dilemmas at every stage of the book's evolution, from the early research through final writing. Our daughter Julia made sure we all had fun throughout.

This book is dedicated to our firstborn, Sophie. She has lived with my writing throughout her twenty years of life to date. I am in awe of the person she is and has become, and am so inspired by her. While I think and write about our nation's troubles, it is Sophie who possesses the capacity and drive to do something about them, to work for change. She is already well on the way, always with her incredible smarts, passion, energy, and style. This book is for her, with deep admiration and boundless love.

Suzanne Mettler
Syracuse, New York
January 2011

NOTES

Introduction

1. Benjamin I. Page and Lawrence R. Jacobs, *Class War?: What Americans Really Think about Economic Inequality* (Chicago: University of Chicago Press, 2009).

2. On the rise of polarization, see Nolan McCarty, Keith T. Poole, and Howard Rosenthal, *Polarized America: The Dance of Ideology and Unequal Riches* (Cambridge, MA: MIT Press, 2006). For more recently updated data, see the Voteview website, http://voteview.com/index.asp. According to the DW-NOMINATE scores, Congress is now more polarized than it has been since the post–Civil War era.

3. Recovery.gov, "Track the Money," http://www.recovery.gov/Pages/home.aspx (accessed October 17, 2010).

4. CBS New/ New York Times Poll 2010, February 5–10, "The Tea Party Movement," http://www.cbsnews.com/htdocs/pdf/poll_Tea_Party_021110.pdf (accessed September 27, 2010); the question read: "So far, do you think the Obama Administration has increased taxes for most Americans, decreased taxes for most Americans, or have they kept taxes the same for most Americans?"

5. Survey conducted by Henry J. Kaiser Family Foundation, April 9–14, 2010, in 1,208 telephone interviews. Available from i-POLL database, Roper Center, http://www.ropercenter.uconn.edu/data_access/ipoll/ipoll.html.

6. Survey by Pew Research Center for the People and the Press, April 1–5, 2010, based on 1,016 telephone interviews. Available from i-POLL database, Roper Center, http://www.ropercenter.uconn.edu/data_access/ipoll/ipoll.html.

7. Philip Rucker, "S.C. Senator Is a Voice of Reform Opposition," *Washington Post*, July 28, 2009, http://www.washingtonpost.com/wp-dyn/content/article/2009/07/27/AR2009072703066.html (accessed October 6, 2010).

8. These figures are drawn from a USA Today/Gallup Poll and a Quinnipiac Poll, both conducted in March 2010. For question wording and a discussion of a larger set of similar questions, see Vanessa Williamson, Theda Skocpol, and John Coggin, "The Tea Party and the Remaking of Republican Conservatism," *Perspectives on Politics* 9, no. 1 (2011): 25–44.

9. "61% Favor Repeal of Health Care Law," *Rasmussen Reports*, September 20, 2010, http://www.rasmussenreports.com/public_content/politics/current_events/healthcare/september_2010/61_favor_repeal_of_health_care_law (accessed December 2, 2010).

10. Gallup Poll, conducted by Gallup Organization, November 6–11, 1936, based on 1,500 personal interviews [USGALLUP.NV2236.R05].

11. Poll conducted by Louis Harris and Associates during December 1965 and based on 1,250 personal interviews. Sample: national adult. As reported in the *Washington Post* [USHARRIS.010966.R2E]. Available from i-POLL database, Roper Center, http://www.ropercenter.uconn.edu/data_access/ipoll/ipoll.html.

12. Karen Orren and Stephen Skowronek, *The Search for American Political Development* (New York: Cambridge University Press, 2004), 20–21.

13. Stephen Skowronek, *Building a New American State: The Expansion of National Administrative Capacities, 1877–1920* (New York: Cambridge University Press, 1982).

14. Suzanne Mettler and Andrew Milstein, "American Political Development from Citizens' Perspective: Tracking Federal Government's Presence in Individual Lives over Time," *Studies in American Political Development* 21 (Spring 2007): 110–30.

15. Readers should try this themselves using any of the available online calculators that rely on IRS data to permit these estimations. I used "Mortgage Tax Deduction Calculator," at Bankrate.com, http://www.bankrate.com/calculators/mortgages/loan-tax-deduction-calculator.aspx (accessed January 12, 2011). In the example provided, the family with an income between $137,301 and $209,250 would receive a benefit of $5,604; $209,250 up to $373,650, a benefit of $6,367.

16. Ronald Reagan, "Inaugural Address, January 20, 1981," in *The American Presidency Project*, by John T. Woolley and Gerhard Peters, http://www.presidency.ucsb.edu/ws/index.php?pid=43130#axzz1Iy2sbRXV (accessed April 8, 2011).

17. Barack Obama, "Announcement for President," February 10, 2007, Springfield, IL, http://www.barackobama.com/2007/02/10/remarks_of_senator_barack_obam_11.php (accessed November 29, 2010); Barack Obama, "Inaugural Address," January 21, 2009, Washington, DC, http://www.whitehouse.gov/blog/inaugural-address/ (accessed November 29, 2010).

18. I am indebted to Larry Jacobs for helping me to understand the argument in these terms.

19. Thomas Piketty and Emmanuel Saez, "Income Inequality in the United States, 1913–1998," *Quarterly Journal of Economics* 118 (February 2003): 1–39.

Chapter One

1. Bill Barrow, "Sen. Mary Landrieu's Health Care Town Hall Meeting Gets Raucous," *Times-Picayune*, August 27, 2009, http://www.nola.com/politics/index.ssf/2009/08/live_from_reserve_sen_mary_lan.html (accessed October 14, 2010).

2. Letters to the Editor, *Columbia Dispatch*, November 30, 2007, 12A.

3. As of 2008, 30 percent of Americans were insured through a government program, and 56 percent received employer-provided health insurance. U.S. Census Bureau, "Table HI01. Health Insurance Coverage Status and Type of Coverage by Selected Characteristics: 2009," *Current Population Survey: Annual Social and Economic Supplement*, http://www.census.gov/hhes/www/cpstables/032010/health/h01_001.htm (accessed October 25, 2010).

4. Elise Gould, "Employer-Sponsored Health Insurance Erosion Accelerates in the Recession: Public Safety Net Catches Kids but Fails to Adequately Insure Adults," *EPI Briefing Paper*, November 16, 2010, Briefing Paper #283, http://www.epi.org/publications/entry/bp283 (accessed December 2, 2010).

5. David Blumenthal and James A. Morone, *The Heart of Power: Health and Politics in the Oval Office* (Berkeley: University of California Press, 2009), 79.

6. U.S. Department of Health and Human Services, Health Resources and Services Administra-

tion, "Am I Eligible?: Health Professions Students," http://www.hrsa.gov/loanscholarships/ students.html (accessed October 31, 2010); U.S. Department of Health and Human Services, Health Resources and Services Administration, "Justification of Estimates for Appropriations Committee, 2011," http://www.hrsa.gov/about/pdf/budgetjust2011.pdf (accessed October 31, 2010).

7. U.S. Department of Health and Human Services, National Health Expenditure Data, "NHE Summary Including Share of GDP: CY 1960–2009," https://www.cms.gov/ nationalhealthexpenddata/02_nationalhealthaccountshistorical.asp (accessed January 12, 2011).

8. Irwin Garfinkel, Lee Rainwater, and Timothy M. Smeeding, "A Re-examination of Welfare States and Inequality in Rich Nations: How In-Kind Transfers and Indirect Taxes Change the Story," *Journal of Policy Analysis and Management* 25, no. 4 (2006): 905; Thomas M. Selden and Merrile Sing, "The Distribution of Public Spending for Health Care in the United States, 2002," *Health Affairs* 29 (July 2008): 353, http://content.healthaffairs.org/cgi/ collection/elderly_collection (accessed December 6, 2010).

9. Lester M. Salamon, "The New Governance and the Tools of Public Action: An Introduction," in *The Tools of Government: A Guide to the New Governance,* ed. Lester M. Salamon (New York: Oxford University Press, 2002), 2.

10. "President's Consumer Panel Studies High Interest Rates on Student Loans," *Washington Post* February 29, 1964, A3.

11. Lawrence E. Gladieux and Thomas R. Wolanin, *Congress and the Colleges: The National Politics of Higher Education* (Lexington, MA: Lexington Books, 1976), 61–62; Thomas H. Stanton and Ronald C. Moe, "Government Corporations and Government-Sponsored Enterprises," in *Tools of Government*, ed. Salamon, 83.

12. Paul Basken, "As 'Crisis' Deters Loan Companies, Direct Lending Sees 43-Percent Jump," *Chronicle of Higher Education*, September 2, 2008.

13. Doug Lederman, "Inside the Cuomo Probe," *Inside Higher Ed*, July 31, 2007, http://www .insidehighered.com/news/2007/07/30/cuomo (accessed January 14, 2011).

14. Social and Governmental Issues and Participation Study of 2008, survey conducted by Survey Research Institute, Cornell University, principal investigator, Suzanne Mettler.

15. Christopher Howard, *The Hidden Welfare State: Tax Expenditures and Social Policy in the United States* (Princeton, NJ: Princeton University Press, 1997), 3, 178.

16. U.S. Budget, *Analytical Perspectives*, FY 2011.

17. Leonard Burman, Eric Toder, and Christopher Geissler, "How Big Are Total Individual Income Tax Expenditures, and Who Benefits from Them?" Discussion Paper No. 31, 2008, Urban-Brookings Tax Policy Center, http://www.taxpolicycenter.org/UploadedPDF/ 1001234_tax_expenditures.pdf (accessed March 1, 2010).

18. U.S. Congressional Budget Office, "A 125-Year Picture of the Federal Government's Share of the Economy, 1950–2075," Long-Range Fiscal Policy Brief, No. 1, July 3, 2002, http://www .cbo.gov/ftpdocs/35xx/doc3521/125RevisedJuly3.pdf (accessed January 10, 2011); U.S. Joint Committee on Taxation, "Estimates of Federal Tax Expenditures for Fiscal Years," various years. See figure 1.2 in this chapter.

19. Quoted in Howard, *Hidden Welfare State*, 4.

20. Survey by Henry J. Kaiser Family Foundation, Harvard School of Public Health, "Kaiser/ Harvard: The Public's Health Care Agenda for the New President and Congress," Methodology: Interviewing conducted by ICR-International Communications Research, De-

cember 4–14, 2008, and based on 1,628 telephone interviews. Sample: national adult [USICR.09HCAGENDA.R27]. The question read: "As you know, most Americans pay taxes on the wages they get from their employers. In cases where an employer also puts money into health insurance benefits for a worker, as far as you know, does the worker pay taxes on the amount the employer puts toward those health care benefits, or not?"

21. Donald F. Kettl, "Performance and Accountability: The Challenge of Government by Proxy for Public Administration," *American Review of Public Administration* 18, no. 1 (March 1988): 9.

22. H. Brinton Milward, "Symposium on the Hollow State: Capacity, Control, and Performance in Interorganizational Settings," *Journal of Public Administration Research and Theory: J-PART* 6, no. 2 (April 1996): 193–95; H. Brinton Milward and Keith G. Provan, "Governing the Hollow State," *Journal of Public Administration Research and Theory: J-PART* 10 no. 2 (2000): 359–79; Howard, *Hidden Welfare State*; Jacob S. Hacker, *The Divided Welfare State: The Battle over Public and Private Social Benefits in the United States* (New York: Cambridge University Press, 2002); Paul C. Light, *The True Size of Government* (Washington, DC: Brookings Institution Press, 1999); Kimberly J. Morgan and Andrea Louise Campbell, "Exploring the Rube Goldberg State" (paper presented at the Annual Meeting of the American Political Science Association, Toronto, Ontario, Canada, September 3–6, 2009).

23. Hacker, *Divided Welfare State*; Howard, *Hidden Welfare State*; Kettl, "Performance and Accountability."

24. Brian Balogh, *A Government Out of Sight: The Mystery of National Authority in Nineteenth-Century America* (New York: Cambridge University Press, 2009); Adam Sheingate, "Why Can't Americans See the State?" *Forum* 7, no. 4 (2009).

25. Kaiser Family Foundation, "Medicare: Medicare Advantage Fact Sheet," September 2010, http://www.kff.org/medicare/upload/2052-14.pdf (accessed November 3, 2010).

26. Rucker, "S.C. Senator Is a Voice of Reform Opposition."

27. See Allison Stanger, *One Nation Under Contract: The Outsourcing of American Power and the Future of Foreign Policy* (New Haven, CT: Yale University Press, 2009); and Sean Farhang, *The Litigation State: Public Regulation and Private Lawsuits in the United States* (Princeton, NJ: Princeton University Press, 2010).

28. Mettler and Milstein, "American Political Development from Citizens' Perspective."

29. Howard, *Hidden Welfare State*, 48–54.

30. Ibid., 176–77.

31. Paul Starr and Gosta Esping-Andersen, "Passive Intervention," *Working Papers for a New Society*, July/August 1979, http://www.princeton.edu/~starr/articles/articles68-79/Starr_Esping-Andersen_Passive_Intervention.pdf (accessed October 19, 2010).

32. Muhammad Attaullah Chaudhry, "The Higher Education Act of 1965: An Historical Case Study" (PhD diss., Oklahoma State University, 1981), 97–99; Jose Chávez, "Presidential Influence on the Politics of Higher Education: The Higher Education Act of 1965" (PhD diss., University of Texas at Austin, 1975), 121–23.

33. Howard, *Hidden Welfare State*, 46, 61, 64–70.

34. Ronald Reagan, "Address to the Nation on the Economy," February 5, 1981, http://www.reagan.utexas.edu/archives/speeches/1981/20581c.htm (accessed February 29, 2011).

35. Quoted in Howard, *Hidden Welfare State*, 190–91.

36. Pete Stark (D-CA), referring to the Targeted Jobs Tax Credit, quoted in Christopher Howard, "Tax Expenditures," in *Tools of Government*, ed. Salamon, 428.

37. Howard, *Hidden Welfare State*, 151–52.

38. Ibid., 179–80.

39. Office of Management and Budget, *Analytical Perspectives: Budget of the United States Government*, FY 1997, 2002, 2007, 2011; Joint Committee on Taxation, "Estimates of Federal Tax Expenditures for Fiscal Years 1990–1994" (1989); Congressional Budget Office, "Tax Expenditures: Current Issues and Five-Year Budget Projections for Fiscal Years 1982–1986" (1981).

40. C. Eugene Steuerle, *Contemporary U.S. Tax Policy*, 2nd ed. (Washington, DC: Urban Institute Press, 2008), 128, 130, 132, 133, 248; Hacker, *Divided Welfare State*, 160–63. Tax reform also increased the standard deduction, so fewer people qualified to itemize deductions.

41. For discussion of patterns of growth over this period, see Eric Toder, "The Changing Composition of Tax Incentives, 1980–99," Urban Institute, http://www.urban.org/publications/410329.html; Burman, Toder, and Geissler, "How Big Are Total Individual Income Tax Expenditures, and Who Benefits From Them?"

42. U.S. Census Bureau, "Annual Social and Economic (ASEC) Supplement" (2005), last modified August 28, 2007, http://pubdb3.census.gov/macro/032007/hhinc/new06_000.htm.

43. Edward L. Glaeser and Jesse M. Shapiro, "The Benefits of the Home Mortgage Interest Deduction," NBER Working Paper no. 9284 (October 2002), http://papers.nber.org/papers/w9284 (accessed October 24, 2010).

44. U.S. Census, "Median and Average Sale Prices of New Homes Sold in the United States," http://www.census.gov/const/uspricemon.pdf (accessed October 20, 2010).

45. Starr and Esping-Andersen, "Passive Intervention."

46. Gould, "Employer-Sponsored Health Insurance Erosion Accelerates in the Recession."

47. Hacker, *Divided Welfare State*, 36–39; Jacob S. Hacker, *The Great Risk Shift: The Assault on American Jobs, Families, Health Care, and Retirement, and How You Can Fight Back* (New York: Oxford University Press, 2006), 139.

48. Gould, "Employer-Sponsored Health Insurance Erosion Accelerates in the Recession."

49. Len Burman, Surachai Khitatrakun, and Sarah Goodell, "Tax Subsidies for Private Health Insurance: Who Benefits and at What Cost?" Robert Wood Johnson Foundation, Synthesis Project, Update, July 2009, http://www.rwjf.org/files/research/072209policysynthesis3update.brief.pdf (accessed January 15, 2011).

50. Frank Levy and Peter Temlin, "Inequality and Institutions in 20th Century America," Industrial Performance Center, MIT, Working Paper Series, MIT-IPC-07-002 (2007), 36–37, http://papers.ssrn.com/sol3/papers.cfm?abstract_id=984330.

51. National Center for Public Policy and Higher Education, *Losing Ground: A National Status Report on the Affordability of American Higher Education* (San Jose, CA: National Center for Public Policy and Higher Education, 2002), 8–9, 12, 22–30.

52. Bethany McLean, "Sallie Mae: A Hot Stock, A Tough Lender," CNNMoney.com, December 14, 2005, http://money.cnn.com/2005/12/14/news/fortune500/sallie_fortune_122605/index.htm (accessed January 29, 2011); "Top 100 Executives by Total Compensation," *Washington Post* (2006), http://projects.washingtonpost.com/post200/2006/executives-by-compensation/ (accessed January 29, 2011).

53. "Fortune 500: Health Care: Insurance and Managed Care, 2009," CNNMoney.com (2010), http://money.cnn.com/magazines/fortune/fortune500/2010/industries/223/index.html (accessed October 25, 2010).

54. Dan Bowman, "2009 Health Insurance CEO Compensation," *Fierce Health Payer*, May 11, 2010,

http://www.fiercehealthpayer.com/special-reports/2009-health-insurance-ceo-compensation (accessed October 28, 2010).

55. Mike Lillis, "Census: Number of Uninsured Americans Skyrocketed Last Year," *The Hill*, September 16, 2010, http://thehill.com/blogs/healthwatch/health-reform-implementation/ 119271-census-number-of-uninsured-americans-skyrocketed-last-year (accessed October 26, 2010).

56. Quoted in Richard W. Stevenson, "The Secret Language of Social Engineering," *New York Times*, July 6, 1997.

57. Andrea Louise Campbell, *How Policies Make Citizens: Senior Political Activism and the American Welfare State* (Princeton, NJ: Princeton University Press, 2003); Suzanne Mettler, *Soldiers to Citizens: The G.I. Bill and the Making of the Greatest Generation* (New York: Oxford University Press, 2005).

58. Mettler, *Soldiers to Citizens*, 7.

59. Skowronek, *Building a New American State*, ix.

60. Michael Grunwald, "How Obama Is Using the Science of Change," *Time*, April 2, 2009; Mike Dorning, "Obama Adopts Behavioral Economics," *Bloomberg Businessweek*, June 24, 2010.

61. "Thaler on Nudging People to Make Better Choices," *Wall Street Journal*, May 13, 2008, http:// blogs.wsj.com/economics/2008/05/13/thaler-on-nudging-people-to-make-better-choices/ (accessed January 29, 2011); Grunwald, "How Obama Is Using the Science of Change."

Chapter Two

1. Jeff Zeleny, "Health Debate Fails to Ignite Obama's Web," *New York Times*, August 15, 2009, A1, A9.

2. Center for Responsive Politics, "Lobbying: Top Spenders, 2009," OpenSecrets.org, http:// www.opensecrets.org/lobby/top.php?showYear=2009&indexType=s (accessed January 31, 2011).

3. E. E. Schattschneider, *Politics, Pressures, and the Tariff: A Study of Free Private Enterprise in Pressure Politics, as Shown in the 1929–1930 Revision of the Tariff* (New York: Prentice-Hall, 1935).

4. Paul Pierson, "When Effect Becomes Cause: Policy Feedback and Political Change," *World Politics* 45, no. 4 (1993): 595–628.

5. Starr and Esping-Andersen, "Passive Intervention."

6. Howard, *Hidden Welfare State*, 104–5.

7. Suzanne Mettler and Deondra Rose, "Unsustainability of Equal Opportunity: The Development of the Higher Education Act of 1965" (paper prepared for delivery at the Annual Meeting of the American Political Science Association, Toronto, Ontario, September 3–6, 2009).

8. The Campaign Finance Institute, "The Cost of Winning an Election, 1986–2010 (in nominal and 2008 dollars)," www.cfinst.org. Federal Election Commission figures for campaigns through 2008 are compiled in Norman J. Ornstein, Thomas E. Mann, and Michael J. Malbin, *Vital Statistics on Congress 2008* (Washington, DC: Brookings Institution Press, 2008), 74.

9. Marian Currinder, Joanne Connor Green, and M. Margaret Conway, "Interest Group Money in Elections," in *Interest Group Politics*, 7th ed., ed. Allan Cigler and Burdett Loomis (Washington, DC: Congressional Quarterly Press, 2007), 182–211.

10. Diana Dwyre, "527s: The New Bad Guys of Campaign Finance," in *Interest Group Politics*, ed. Cigler and Loomis, 212–32.

11. Author's interviews with members of the higher education policy community (including lobbyists and staff for lenders and trade associations, congressional staff, agency officials, and representatives of student organizations), Washington, DC, April–May 2010 (hereafter "Author's Interviews 2010").

12. Theda Skocpol, *Diminished Democracy: From Membership to Management in American Civic Life* (Norman: University of Oklahoma Press, 2003); Jeffrey M. Berry, *The New Liberalism: The Rising Power of Citizen Groups* (Washington, DC: Brookings Institution Press, 1993).

13. Howard, *Hidden Welfare State*, 9, 114–15, 181; Suzanne Mettler, "Visible Lessons: How Experiences of Higher Education Policies Influence Participation in Politics," unpublished paper, 2009.

14. Marie Gottschalk, *The Shadow Welfare State: Labor, Business, and the Politics of Health Care in the United States* (Ithaca, NY: Cornell University Press, 2000); Andrea Louise Campbell and Theda Skocpol, "AARP at Risk of Medicare Blowback," *Albany Times Union*, November 30, 2003 (originally written for *Newsday*), http://www.nysaaaa.org/News%20Headlines/Editorial_Medicare_TU_12-03-03.pdf (accessed March 1, 2010).

15. Burdett A. Loomis, "Does K Street Run through Capitol Hill?: Lobbying Congress in the Republican Era," in *Interest Group Politics*, ed. Cigler and Loomis, 412–30.

16. Barbara Sinclair, *Party Wars: Polarization and the Politics of National Policy Making* (Norman: University of Oklahoma Press, 2006), 308–14.

17. Richard L. Hall and Frank W. Wayman, "Buying Time: Moneyed Interests and the Mobilization of Bias in Congressional Committees," *American Political Science Review* 84, no. 3 (1990): 797–820.

18. Stephen Ansolabehere, John M. de Figueiredo, and James M. Snyder Jr., "Why Is There So Little Money in U.S. Politics?" *Journal of Economic Perspectives* 17, no. 1 (Winter 2003): 105–30.

19. The concept of policy visibility is developed in Pierson, "When Effect Becomes Cause"; Salamon, "The New Governance and the Tools of Public Action"; and R. Douglas Arnold, *The Logic of Congressional Action* (New Haven, CT: Yale University Press, 1990), 47–51.

20. The full name of the Governmental Issues Survey is the Social and Governmental Issues and Participation Study of 2008. It consisted of a telephone survey of 1,400 Americans, including a national random sample of 1,000 plus oversamples of 200 low-income individuals and 200 individuals ages 25–34. It was conducted by the Cornell Survey Research Institute, from August 23–November 1, 2008. The response rate was 34 percent, calculated according to AAPOR guidelines. Data in author's possession; to be made publicly available as of 2015.

21. Mettler and Milstein, "American Political Development from Citizens' Perspective," 112–13. I have calculated average monthly benefits as average annual benefits by multiplying by twelve.

22. Sandy Baum and Marie O'Malley, "College on Credit: How Borrowers Perceive Their Education Debt, Results of the 2002 National Student Loan Survey," Final Report, February 6, 2003 (conducted for Nellie Mae Corporation), http://www.nelliemae.com/library/research_10.html. Average student borrower borrowed $18,900 for her studies; I have divided this figure by four, signifying years of undergraduate study, to produce an average annual figure.

23. Governmental Issues Survey, 2008.

24. See Mettler and Milstein, "American Political Development from Citizens' Perspective," 121, fig. 7, with amounts calculated as annual benefits.

25. Mark Leff, "Taxing the 'Forgotten Man': The Politics of Social Security Finance in the New Deal," *Journal of American History* 70 (September 1983): 359–81; Edwin E. Witte, *Development of the Social Security Act* (Madison: University of Wisconsin Press, 1962), 149–50.

26. Rucker, "S.C. Senator Is a Voice of Reform Opposition."

27. Mettler, *Soldiers to Citizens*. Further exploration of policy visibility appears in Mettler, "Visible Lessons"; and Julianna Koch and Suzanne Mettler, "Who Perceives Government's Role in Their Lives?: How Policy Visibility Influences Awareness and Attitudes about Social Spending," paper presented at the Annual Meeting of the Midwest Political Science Association, Chicago, IL, March 31–April 3, 2011.

28. New York Times, "Polling the Tea Party: Survey Report," April 14, 2010, http://www.nytimes.com/interactive/2010/04/14/us/politics/20100414-tea-party-poll-graphic.html#tab=3 (accessed January 30, 2011); CBS News Poll/New York Times, "The Tea Party Movement: What They Think," April 5–12, 2010, http://www.cbsnews.com/htdocs/pdf/poll_tea_party_041410.pdf?tag=contentMain;contentBody (accessed January 30, 2011).

29. Kate Zernike and Megan Thee-Brenan, "Poll Finds Tea Party Backers Wealthier and More Educated," April 14, 2010, http://www.nytimes.com/2010/04/15/us/politics/15poll.html (accessed January 29, 2011).

30. Joe Soss, "Lessons of Welfare: Policy Design, Political Learning, and Political Action," *American Political Science Review* 93 (1999): 363–80.

31. It should be noted that these cross-sectional data do not allow us to make causal inferences with certainty, for reasons to be discussed in chapter 3. Here we will observe correlations between variables.

32. The Earned Income Tax Credit is not included in this analysis both because it is designed in a way that appears to make its existence as a social benefit more apparent, given that those without tax liability may claim it, and because organizations have publicized its availability in low-income communities in recent years and helped eligible individuals to claim it.

33. The analysis in this paragraph and those following was conducted using the data for the Governmental Issues Survey, 2008.

34. Ordinary least squares regression results with "government programs have helped me" (from "disagree strongly" to "agree strongly") as the dependent variable yielded the following results (standardized coefficients and significance, $*p < .10$; $**p < .05$; $***p < .01$, $****p < .001$ [two-sided]): sum of direct federal social programs ever used, .34****; African American, −.03; Hispanic, .02; year of birth, .07**; income, −.06*; education, −.04; female, −.04. Adjusted R^2, .13; $N = 1,243$.

35. Ordinary least squares regression results with "government programs helped" (from "disagree strongly" to "agree strongly") as the dependent variable yielded the following results (standardized coefficients and significance, $*p < .10$; $**p < .05$; $***p < .01$, $****p < .001$ [two-sided]): sum of tax expenditures ever used out of four, .01; African American, .04; Hispanic, .01; year of birth, .02; income, −.20****; education, −.13; female, −.01; adjusted R^2, .04; $N = 1,237$. In the next model, the sum of tax expenditures was replaced by employer-sponsored savings plan for retirement dummy variable, −.04; other results comparable, adjusted R^2, .04, $N = 1,224$. In the final model, the sum of tax expenditures was replaced by having health insurance plan through employer dummy variable, −.02; other results comparable, adjusted R^2, .04, $N = 1,235$.

36. Ordinary least squares regression results with "government has given me opportunities to improve my standard of living" (from "disagree strongly" to "agree strongly") as the dependent variable yielded the following results (standardized coefficients and significance, $*p < .10$; $**p < .05$; $***p < .01$, $****p < .001$ [two-sided]): sum of direct federal social programs ever used, $.09***$; African American, $-.04$; Hispanic, $.06*$; year of birth, $-.06**$; income, $-.01$; education, $.07**$; female, $-.09***$. Adjusted R^2, $.02$; $N = 1,262$.

37. Ordinary least squares regression results with "government has given me opportunities to improve my standard of living" (from "disagree strongly" to "agree strongly") as the dependent variable yielded the following results (standardized coefficients and significance, $*p < .10$; $**p < .05$; $***p < .01$, $****p < .001$ [two-sided]): sum of tax expenditures ever used out of four, $-.07**$; African American, $-.18$; Hispanic, $.05*$; year of birth, $-07**$; income, $-.03$; education, $.09**$; female, $-.01**$. Adjusted R^2, $.02$; $N = 1,256$. In another model, sum of tax expenditures was replaced by employer-sponsored savings plan for retirement dummy variable, $-.02$; other results comparable, adjusted R^2, $.02$, $N = 1,244$. In additional model, sum of tax expenditures was replaced by having health insurance plan through employer dummy variable, $-.02$; other results comparable, adjusted R^2, $.04$, $N = 1,254$.

38. Of the remainder, 3 percent said they paid less than their "fair share," and 1 percent explained that they do not pay taxes.

39. Ordinary least squares regression results with feelings about whether asked to pay fair share in federal income taxes (from "asked to pay more than fair share" to "asked to pay less than fair share") as the dependent variable yielded the following results (standardized coefficients and significance, $*p < .10$; $**p < .05$; $***p < .01$, $****p < .001$ [two-sided]): sum of tax expenditures ever used out of four, $-.03$; African American, $-.15****$; Hispanic, $-.06*$; year of birth, $-.02$; income, $-.14****$; education, $.11****$; female, $-.12****$. Adjusted R^2, $.05$; $N = 1,249$.

40. In an employer-provided health insurance variant of the tax-fairness model described in note 38, the sum of tax expenditures was replaced by employer-provided health insurance, $-.03$; other results comparable to those in note 38; adjusted R^2, $.05$, $N = 1,247$. In an additional model, the sum of tax expenditures was replaced by having employer-sponsored savings plan for retirement, dummy variable, $-.02$; other results comparable, adjusted R^2, $.04$, $N = 1,236$.

41. In an additional model of determinants of view about tax fairness, I substituted the variable "sum of direct federal social programs ever used" for the policy variable and kept other aspects of the model the same as described in notes 38 and 39. Standardized coefficient for policy variable: $.07**$; all other results comparable to above; adjusted R^2, $.05$, $N = 1,255$.

42. Steven J. Rosenstone and John Mark Hansen, *Mobilization, Participation, and Democracy in America* (New York: Macmillan, 1993), 108–9, 115, 117; Campbell, *How Policies Make Citizens*, 36–37, and passim.

43. I am indebted to Helen Ingram for influencing me to think about the degenerative feedback effects of some policies.

Chapter Three

1. Michael Cooper, "From Obama, the Tax Cut Nobody Heard Of," *New York Times*, October 18, 2010, A1, A18.

2. James Surowiecki, "A Smarter Stimulus," *New Yorker*, January 26, 2009, http://www

.newyorker.com/talk/financial/2009/01/26/090126ta_talk_surowiecki (accessed October 29, 2010).

3. Cooper, "From Obama, the Tax Cut Nobody Heard Of."

4. Ibid.

5. Richard Thaler and Sendhil Mullainathan, "How Behavioral Economics Differs from Traditional Economics," *The Concise Encyclopedia of Economics* (2008), http://www.econlib.org/library/Enc/BehavioralEconomics.html (accessed October 28, 2010); Craig Lambert, "The Marketplace of Perceptions," *Harvard Magazine*, March–April 2006, 50–57, 93–95; Grunwald, "How Obama Is Using the Science of Change."

6. Richard H. Thaler and Cass R. Sunstein, *Nudge: Improving Decisions about Health, Wealth, and Happiness* (New York: Penguin Books, 2009), 3–14.

7. Ibid., 109–12.

8. Grunwald, "How Obama Is Using the Science of Change."

9. Quoted in Lambert, "The Marketplace of Perceptions," 57.

10. Eric P. Bettinger, Bridget Terry Long, Philip Oreopoulos, and Lisa Sanbonmatsu, "The Role of Simplification and Information in College Decisions: Results from the H&R Block FAFSA Experiment," September 2009, Working Paper 15361, National Bureau of Economic Research, http://www.nber.org/papers/w15361 (accessed January 29, 2011).

11. For a fuller discussion, see Donald R. Kinder and Thomas R. Palfrey, "On Behalf of an Experimental Political Science," in *Experimental Foundations of Political Science*, ed. Donald R. Kinder and Thomas R. Palfrey (Ann Arbor: University of Michigan Press, 1993), 1–37; Donald P. Green and Alan S. Gerber, "Reclaiming the Experimental Tradition in Political Science," in *Political Science: The State of the Discipline*, ed. Ira Katznelson and Helen Milner (New York: Norton, 2003), 805–33.

12. Donald P. Green and Alan S. Gerber, "Recent Advances in the Science of Voter Mobilization," in "The Science of Voter Mobilization," special issue, *Annals of the American Academy of Political and Social Science* 601 (September 2005): 6–9.

13. Diana C. Mutz, "Cross-Cutting Social Networks: Testing Democratic Theory in Practice," *American Political Science Review* 96 (March 2002): 122.

14. Exceptions include Jennifer Jerit, "How Predictive Appeals Affect Policy Opinions," *American Journal of Political Science* 53 (2009): 411–26; and Richard R. Lau and Marc Schlesinger, *Political Psychology* 26 (2005): 77–114.

15. National Public Radio, "Americans' Views on Taxes: An NPR/Kaiser Family Foundation/Kennedy School of Government Poll" (2003), http://www.npr.org/news/specials/polls/taxes2003/index.html (accessed January 8, 2007).

16. Angus Campbell, Philip Converse, Warren Miller, and Donald Stokes, *The American Voter* (New York: Wiley; 1964); Philip E. Converse, "The Nature of Belief Systems in Mass Publics," in *Ideology and Discontent*, ed. David E. Apter (New York: Free Press), 206–61.

17. For example, Lawrence R. Jacobs and Robert Y. Shapiro, *Politicians Don't Pander: Political Manipulation and the Loss of Democratic Responsiveness* (Chicago: University of Chicago Press, 2000); James N. Druckman, "Political Preference Formation: Competition, Deliberation, and the (Ir)relevance of Framing Effects," *American Political Science Review* 98 (2004): 671–86.

18. For a useful discussion about how voters process political information, with a particular focus on tax policy, see Larry M. Bartels, *Unequal Democracy: The Political Economy of the New Gilded Age* (Princeton, NJ: Princeton University Press and Russell Sage Foundation, 2008), 162–96. Also see Brendan Nyhan and Jason Reifler, "When Corrections Fail: the Per-

sistence of Political Misperceptions," *Political Behavior* 32, no. 2 (2010): 303–30; Charles S. Taber and Milton Lodge, "Motivated Skepticism in the Evaluation of Political Beliefs," *American Journal of Political Science* 50 (2006): 755–69; and Brian J. Gaines, James H. Kuklinski, Paul J. Quirk, Buddy Peyton, and Jay Verkuilen, "Same Facts, Different Interpretations: Partisan Motivation and Opinion on Iraq," *Journal of Politics* 69 (2007): 957–74.

19. Hacker, *Divided Welfare State*, 9.

20. John R. Zaller, *The Nature and Origins of Mass Opinion* (New York: Cambridge University Press, 1992); Michael X. Delli Carpini and Scott Keeter, *What Americans Know about Politics and Why It Matters* (New Haven, CT: Yale University Press, 1996); Scott L. Althaus, "Information Effects in Collective Preferences," *American Political Science Review* 92, no. 3 (1998): 545–58.

21. Vincent Price and John R. Zaller, "Who Gets the News?: Alternative Measures of News Reception and Their Implications for Research," *Public Opinion Quarterly* 57, no. 2 (2003): 133–64.

22. Delli Carpini and Keeter, *What Americans Know*.

23. Martin Gilens, "Political Ignorance and Collective Policy Preferences," *American Political Science Review* 95, no. 2 (2001): 379–96.

24. The experiment was administered through Time-Sharing Experiments for the Social Sciences (TESS), which is supported by the National Science Foundation. The actual survey was conducted by Knowledge Networks. This firm uses a random-digit dialing method to obtain a representative general population sample. Subjects who agree to participate in TESS projects receive free access to the Internet via WebTV for as long as they remain in the sample. The response rate was 63.1 percent, calculated according to the American Association for Public Opinion Research Approach #3. Our survey was in the field February 21–28, 2008.

25. This approach permits us to examine how the same subjects' levels of policy support were influenced by different types and amounts of information. It also has the advantage of increasing the number of research subjects experiencing the same condition, thus elevating statistical power and reducing results of individual variance.

26. Treatments for the other two policies, each of which follows the same form, are summarized in the appendix.

27. The experiment also included one more treatment that we do not discuss here because of space limitation. It was the "two-stage" treatment, in which participants received the basic policy description up front, before being asked their view of the policy for the first time, and then they were told the distributive effects, and then asked their support a second time. See Suzanne Mettler and Matt Guardino, "Revealing the 'Hidden Welfare State': How Policy Information Influences Public Attitudes about Tax Expenditures," unpublished paper, available from author.

28. In order to simplify the presentation in table 3.1, we collapsed the response categories "favor strongly" and "favor somewhat" into a single "favor" category, and the categories "oppose strongly" and "oppose somewhat" into a single "oppose" category. The results are not sensitive to this presentation.

29. In all six experiments, the reduction in the number of respondents answering "don't know" was highly significant, at the $p < .001$ level, as indicated by paired t-tests.

30. These changes in level of support achieved statistical significance only in the case of the HMID, which generated a t-value of -2.48, $p < .05$.

31. Ann L. Schneider and Helen M. Ingram, *Policy Design for Democracy* (Lawrence: University of Kansas Press, 1997).

32. U.S. Census, "More Householders than Ever Own Their Own Homes According to Census 2000," press release (2001), http://www.census.gov/Press-Release/www/releases/archives/housing/000537.html (accessed March 28, 2008).

33. The changes in support for the two upwardly distributive policies were highly significant, $p < .001$, based on paired t-tests.

34. This difference can perhaps be explained by the fact that the basic information treatment for the EITC already provided some distributive information, noting that the policy was geared to "people who work but do not make much money." This information, which was included because we judged it to be an integral part of the basic description of the policy, may be responsible for the relatively modest increase in support following the full information treatment.

35. Delli Carpini and Keeter, *What Americans Know*, 157.

36. Zaller, *Nature and Origins*; Gilens, "Political Ignorance and Collective Policy Preferences."

37. The additional questions were "What job or political office is now held by Dick Cheney?"; "How much of a majority is required for the U.S. Senate and House to override a presidential veto?"; and "[Is] one of the major parties more conservative than the other at the national level? If so, which . . . ?"

38. We categorized as "high knowledge" subjects who answered four or five questions correctly, as "moderate" those who answered two or three items correctly, and as "low" subjects who answered zero or one question right.

39. The magnitude of this change reached the level of statistical significance in fifteen out of the eighteen cases.

40. Full results with significance levels are available from the author.

41. For example, Zaller, *Nature and Origins*, 118–24.

42. This question read, "Do you or does anyone in your household benefit from any of the following policies? Please check 'yes,' 'no,' or 'don't know' for each."

43. Delli Carpini and Keeter, *What Americans Know*, chaps. 4–5.

44. Annual household incomes up to $34,999 were defined as low; $35,000 to $74,999 as middle; and $75,000 and above as high.

45. Because we examined the effects of specific policy information on the propensity to articulate opinions in the previous section, these graphs omit "don't know/no opinion" responses. Thus, the percentages in each set of columns do not sum to 100. In addition, we added the responses for "favor strongly" and "favor somewhat," and "oppose strongly" and "oppose somewhat," respectively, to create two broad categories labeled "favor" and "oppose."

46. Statistical significance of differences in responses pre- and post-treatment are indicated by the following t-values, with significance reported as ***$p < .001$, **$p < .01$: low income, 6.73***; medium, 2.75**; high, .74.

47. Statistical significance of differences in responses pre- and post-treatment are indicated by the following t-values, with significance reported as ***$p < .001$, **$p < .01$: low income, 5.30***; medium, 3.09**; high, 1.20.

48. Statistical significance of differences in responses pre- and post-treatment are indicated by the following t-values, with significance reported as ***$p < .001$, **$p < .01$: low income, −1.47; medium, −.06; high, −1.19.

49. Page and Jacobs, *Class War?*, 144.

50. Andrew Gelman, Boris Shor, Joseph Bafumi, and David Park, "Rich State, Poor State, Red State, Blue State: What's the Matter with Connecticut?" *Quarterly Journal of Political Science* 2 (2007): 345.

51. John Sides, "Stories, Science, and Public Opinion about the Estate Tax," June 2010, paper posted at the Monkey Cage, http://home.gwu.edu/~jsides/estatetax.pdf (accessed November 17, 2010).

52. I did not manage to find a typescript copy of the speech I heard that night. Similar language appeared, however, in Barack Obama, "Tax Fairness for the Middle Class," Washington, DC, September 18, 2007, http://www.barackobama.com/2007/09/18/remarks_of _senator_barack_obam_25.php (accessed January 29, 2011).

Chapter Four

1. Barack Obama, "Remarks by the President on Higher Education," White House, Office of the Press Secretary, April 24, 2009, http://www.whitehouse.gov/the_press_office/ Remarks-by-the-President-on-Higher-Education/ (accessed September 21, 2009).

2. Ibid.

3. For example, David H. Garrison, "Government Takeover of Student Loans Is a Bad Idea," *Washington Examiner*, December 21, 2009, http://washingtonexaminer.com/node/ 136481 (accessed January 30, 2011); Dana Perino, "Beware of Democrats' Other Public Option," *Fox News*, January 15, 2010, http://www.foxnews.com/opinion/2010/01/15/ dana-perino-student-loans-public-option-harkin-democrats/ (accessed January 30, 2011); Walter Alarkon, "Beneficiaries of Sallie Mae, Nelnet Fight Obama's Student-Aid Proposal," *The Hill*, March 9, 2009.

4. Author's Interviews 2010.

5. OECD 2007, "Education at a Glance: OECD Briefing Note for the United States," www.oecd .org/edu/eag2007 (accessed January 29, 2011).

6. College Board, "Trends in Student Aid 2004," Trends in Higher Education Series, www .collegeboard.com; Jacqueline E. King, *2000 Status Report on the Pell Grant Program* (American Council on Education, Center for Policy Analysis, 2000), 9–10.

7. OECD, "Education at a Glance." For analyses of why college graduation rates have not improved more among less advantaged young people, see Thomas J. Kane, *The Price of Admission: Rethinking How Americans Pay for College* (New York: Russell Sage Foundation, 1999); Claudia Goldin and Lawrence F. Katz, *The Race between Technology and Education* (Cambridge, MA: Harvard University Press, 2008); and Donald E. Heller, *Condition of Access: Higher Education for Lower Income Students* (Westport, CT: Praeger, 2002).

8. Tom Mortenson, "Bachelor's Degree Attainment by Age 24 by Family Income Quartiles, 1970 to 2007" (2005, 2007), data in author's possession, available from Postsecondary Education Opportunity, www.postsecondary.org.

9. Barack Obama, "Remarks of Senator Barack Obama: Reclaiming the American Dream," Bettendorf, IA, November 7, 2007, http://www.barackobama.com/2007/11/07/ remarks_of_senator_barack_obam_31.php (accessed September 18, 2009).

10. Barack Obama, "Remarks of President Barack Obama—Address to Joint Session of Congress," February 24, 2009, http://www.whitehouse.gov/the_press_office/ Remarks-of-President-Barack-Obama-Address-to-Joint-Session-of-Congress/ (accessed September 19, 2009).

11. Lawrence E. Gladiuex and Arthur M. Hauptman, *The College Aid Quandary: Access, Quality, and the Federal Role* (Washington, DC: Brookings Institution, 1995).

12. Project on Student Debt, "Student Debt and the Class of 2009," October 2009, http://projectonstudentdebt.org/files/pub/classof2009.pdf (accessed January 30, 2011).

13. Derek V. Price, *Borrowing Inequality: Race, Class, and Student Loans* (Boulder, CO: Lynne Rienner Publishers, 2004).

14. Scott Jaschik, "Bankers Descend on Capitol Hill," *Chronicle of Higher Education*, March 10, 1993; Jim Zook, "Stock Hits New Low: Sallie Mae Fights Direct Lending Plan," *Chronicle of Higher Education*, February 24, 1993.

15. "Student Loan Changes," *CQ Almanac* (1986): 268; "Action Postponed on Student-Loan Defaults," *CQ Almanac* (1986): 340.

16. Author's Interviews 2010; author's interviews with members of the higher education policy community (including lobbyists and staff for lenders and trade associations, congressional staff, agency officials, and representatives of student organizations), Washington, DC, Fall 2007 (hereafter "Author's Interviews 2007").

17. Center for Responsive Politics, "PACS, Finance/Credit Companies: PAC Contributions to Federal Candidates, Election Cycle 2008," OpenSecrets.org, http://www.opensecrets.org/pacs/industry.php?txt=F06&cycle=2008 (accessed April 12, 2011).

18. Center for Responsive Politics, "Lobbying, Finance/Credit Companies, Industry Profile 2007," OpenSecrets.org, http://www.opensecrets.org/lobby/indusclient.php?year=2007&lname=F06&id= (accessed April 12, 2011).

19. Author's Interviews 2007, 2010.

20. Jason Delisle, "Student Loan Purchase Programs under the Ensuring Continued Access to Student Loans Act of 2008," Issue Brief, New America Foundation (2009), http://www.newamerica.net/publications/policy/student_loan_purchase_programs_under_ensuring_continued_access_student_loans_act_2008_0 (accessed May 19, 2010).

21. Author's Interviews 2010.

22. Troy Onink, "The New Improved College Tax Credit," *Forbes*, March 10, 2009.

23. OMB, Analytical Perspectives, FY 2011, http://www.whitehouse.gov/sites/default/files/omb/budget/fy2011/assets/receipts.pdf (accessed January 29, 2011); U.S. Department of Education, "Federal Pell Grant Program," http://www2.ed.gov/programs/fpg/funding.html (accessed January 29, 2011).

24. Susan Dynarski, "Hope for Whom?: Financial Aid for the Middle Class and Its Impact on College Attendance," *National Tax Journal* 53 (2000): 629–62; Bridget Terry Long, "The Impact of Federal Tax Credits for Higher Education Expenses," NBER Working Paper No. w9553, JEL NO. I2, H2, (2003), 1–70; Author's Interviews 2010.

25. Doug Lederman, "Big Savings from Loan Proposal," *Inside Higher Ed*, March 23, 2009.

26. Author's Interviews 2010.

27. David M. Herszenhorn, "Obama Student Loan Plan Wins Support in House," *New York Times*, September 10, 2009.

28. Six Republicans joined Democrats in support, and four Democrats allied with Republicans in opposition.

29. Doug Lederman, "Aid Bill Moves, Amid Misgivings," *Inside Higher Ed*, July 22, 2009.

30. Lederman, "Aid Bill Moves, Amid Misgivings."

31. The stimulus bill devoted $15.6 billion to the Pell Grant program. It improved their availability, with the aim of reaching seven million low- and moderate-income individu-

als, and boosted maximum grant levels up from $4,731 to $5,550. U.S. Congress, 111th Cong., 1st Sess., "H.R. 1 An Act Making supplemental appropriations for job preservation and creation, infrastructure investment, energy efficiency and science, assistance to the unemployed, and State and local fiscal stabilization, for the fiscal year ending September 30, 2009, and for other purposes" (2009), http://frwebgate.access.gpo.gov/cgi-bin/getdoc .cgi?dbname=111_cong_bills&docid=f:h1enr.pdf (accessed September 19, 2009); U.S. Department of Education, "The American Recovery and Reinvestment Act of 2009: Education Jobs and Reform," February 18, 2009, http://www.ed.gov/policy/gen/leg/recovery/ factsheet/overview.html (accessed September 19, 2009); "Details of the Stimulus Plan," *CQ Weekly*, January 19, 2009, 127.

32. Tamar Lewin, "House Passes Bill to Expand College Aid," *New York Times*, September 18, 2009; Kelly Field, "Houses Passes Bill to End Bank-Based Lending," *Chronicle of Higher Education*, September 17, 2009; Doug Lederman, "House Passes Student Aid Bill," *Inside Higher Ed*, September 18, 2009; U.S. Congress, "Student Aid and Fiscal Responsibility Act of 2009," *Congressional Record* 155 (September 16, 2009): H9594–637.

33. Ed Howard, "Nelson Cited as 'Emblematic' of Administration's Problems," *Nebraska State Paper*, April 1, 2009, http://nebraska.statepaper.com/vnews/display.v/ART/2009/04/01/ 49d355604df9c (accessed September 21, 2009).

34. Josh Gerstein, "Dems Take Aim at W.H. on Student Loans," *Politico*, March 25, 2009.

35. Sinclair, *Party Wars*.

36. Kelly Field, "Congress Is Poised to Ease Passage of Obama's Plan to End Bank-Based Lending," *Chronicle of Higher Education*, April 27, 2009.

37. Author's Interviews 2010.

38. Field, "Congress Is Poised to Ease Passage of Obama's Plan."

39. Alarkon, "Beneficiaries of Sallie Mae, Nelnet Fight Obama's Student-Aid Proposal"; Danielle Knight, "Lobbying Showdown over the Future of Student Loans," *Huffington Post*, July 29, 2009, http://www.huffingtonpost.com/2009/07/29/lobbying-showdown-over-th_n_247506 .html (accessed September 21, 2009); Maryann Dreas, "Private Lenders Focus on Jobs in Student Loan Fight," *The Hill*, November 30, 2009, http://thehill.com/business-a-lobbying/ 69873-private-lenders-focus-on-jobs-in-student-loan-fight (accessed January 30, 2011).

40. Dreas, "Private Lenders Focus on Jobs."

41. Corey Boles, "Alternate Senate Student Loan Plan Would Retain Role for Banks," *Dow Jones News Wire*, December 2, 2009, http://www.advfn.com/news_Alternate-Senate-Student -Loan-Plan-Would-Retain-Role-For-Banks_40615283.html (accessed January 30, 2011).

42. Author's Interviews 2010; author's interviews with members of the higher education policy community (including lobbyists and staff for lenders and trade associations, congressional staff, agency officials, and representatives of student organizations), Washington, DC, January 2011 (hereafter "Author's Interviews 2011")

43. Ibid.

44. U.S. Bureau of Labor Statistics, "Union Members—2010," January 2011, http://www.bls.gov/ news.release/union2.nr0.htm (accessed January 30, 2011).

45. Figure 4.1 was created from a content analysis of speeches on health care, taxes, and higher education by Barack Obama (not White House staff) between January 2009 and March 21, 2010. Included are including those categorized as "Speeches and Remarks" and "Your Weekly Address," available on White House Briefing Room, http://www.whitehouse.gov/ briefing-room. Health speeches include those during which Obama mentions or discusses

health reform. Tax speeches include those during which Obama mentions or discusses tax cuts, tax credits, or tax expenditures (e.g., limiting the itemized deduction). Higher education speeches include those during which Obama mentions or discusses higher education, particularly education tax credits (American Opportunity Tax Credit), Pell Grants, student loans, and community colleges. Some speeches are included in multiple categories. For example, discussions of the American Opportunity Tax Credit are included in both the tax category and the higher education category. Mentions of the limit on itemized deductions are included in both the health category (as a financing option for the overhaul) and in the tax category. These same procedures were used to generate the individual policy area graphs in figures 4.2, 5.1, and 5.2. Coding available from the author.

46. For source and coding information, see note 45.
47. Barack Obama, "Remarks by the President in the State of the Union Address," January 27, 2010, http://www.whitehouse.gov/the-press-office/remarks-president-state-union-address (accessed April 11, 2011).
48. Author's Interviews 2010; Doug Lederman, "What Now for Student Aid Bill?" *Inside Higher Ed*, March 8, 2010; Daniel De Vise, "House Approves Huge Changes to Student Loan Program," *Washington Post*, March 22, 2010.
49. Jason Delisle, "Senator Conrad's Choice on Student Loan Bill," *Higher Ed Watch*, New America Foundation, January 19, 2010, http://higheredwatch.newamerica.net/blogposts/2010/senator_conrads_choice_on_student_loan_bill-26445 (accessed May 19, 2010).
50. Author's Interviews 2010; Manu Raju and Glenn Thrush, "Conrad, Dems Split in Loan Spat," *Politico* March 19, 2010. The letter was signed by senators Thomas Carper (DE), Blanche Lincoln (AR), Ben Nelson (NE), Bill Nelson (FL), Mark Warner (VA), and Jim Webb (VA); David M. Herszenhorn, "Obama's Student Loan Overhaul Endangered," *New York Times*, March 10, 2010.
51. Paul Basken, "Student-Loan Bill Begins Showdown Week," *Chronicle of Higher Education*, March 15, 2010.
52. Paul Basken, "Historic Victory for Student Aid Is Tinged by Lost Possibilities," *Chronicle of Higher Education*, March 25, 2010; Author's Interviews 2010.
53. Paul Basken, "Minority-Serving Colleges Benefit from a Student-Loan Change They Fought," *Chronicle of Higher Education*, April 4, 2010.
54. Author's Interviews 2010.
55. Ibid.
56. Kevin Carey, "Taking an Incomplete: The Disastrous Education Compromise that Marred Obama's Best Week in Office," *New Republic*, April 13, 2010.
57. Author's Interviews 2010.
58. Suzanne Mettler, "Promoting Inequality: The Politics of Higher Education Policy in an Era of Conservative Governance," in *The Unsustainable American State*, ed. Lawrence Jacobs and Desmond King (New York: Oxford University Press, 2010), 197–222.

Chapter Five

1. Jeff Zeleny, "Blogging the Massachusetts Senate Race," *The Caucus: The Politics and Government Blog of the Times*, January 19, 2010, http://thecaucus.blogs.nytimes.com/2010/01/19/blogging-the-mass-senate-race/ (accessed April 8, 2011).
2. Survey by NBC News, Wall Street Journal, October 22–25, 2009, [USNBCWSJ.09OCT.

R35BA], available from i-POLL database, Roper Center, http://www.ropercenter.uconn
.edu/data_access/ipoll/ipoll.html.

3. Survey by Henry J. Kaiser Family Foundation, February 11–16, 2010, [USPSRA.10HTPFEB.
R04D], available from i-POLL database, Roper Center, http://www.ropercenter.uconn.edu/
data_access/ipoll/ipoll.html.

4. Survey by CBS News Poll, March 29–April 1, 2010, [USCBS.040210A.R14], available from
i-POLL database, Roper Center, http://www.ropercenter.uconn.edu/data_access/ipoll/ipoll
.html.

5. Joseph J. Schatz, "Obama's Budget Proposal Alters the Typical Tax and Spend Equation," *CQ Weekly*, March 2, 2009, 480–81; Tax Policy Center, "Major Provisions of the
McCain and Obama Tax Plans" (2008), http://www.taxpolicycenter.org/tpccontent/
tax_plan_matrix_0608.pdf (accessed January 29, 2011).

6. Howard, *Hidden Welfare State*, 109–12.

7. Albert B. Crenshaw, "Higher Income Benefits Fade," *Washington Post*, February 26, 2006,
http://www.washingtonpost.com/wp-dyn/content/article/2006/02/25/AR2006022500249
.html (accessed March 1, 2010); Aviva Aron-Dine and Robert Greenstein, "Two High
Income Tax Cuts Not Yet Fully in Effect Will Cost Billions over the Next Five Years,"
Center on Budget and Policy Priorities, February 1, 2007, http://www.cbpp.org/cms/
?fa=view&id=1041 (accessed March 1, 2010); Tax Policy Center, "Selected Provisions of Major Tax Legislation by Effective Date 1981–2011," August 2010, http://www.taxpolicycenter
.org/legislation/upload/legislation_by_date.pdf (accessed January 29, 2011).

8. Barack Obama, "Address on Tax Fairness for the Middle Class," September 18, 2007, http://
www.barackobama.com/2007/09/18/remarks_of_senator_barack_obam_25.php (accessed
March 1, 2010).

9. Lily L. Batchelder, Fred T. Goldberg Jr., and Peter R. Orszag, "Efficiency and Tax Incentives:
The Case for Refundable Tax Credits," *Stanford Law Review* 59 (2006): 23–76.

10. On these New Deal programs, see Arthur M. Schlesinger, *The Coming of the New Deal: The
Age of Roosevelt*, Vol. 2, *1933–1935* (New York: Houghton Mifflin, 1958), 270–71, 337–41. My
observation about Americans' memories of such policies is based on my own interviews
with World War II veterans, conducted in 1998–2000, and also from reports from interviews with grandparents conducted by undergraduates in my public policy courses.

11. "Track the Money," Recovery.gov, http://www.recovery.gov/Pages/home.aspx (accessed
January 23, 2010).

12. U.S. Senate Finance and House Ways and Means Committee, "The American Recovery and
Reinvestment Act of 2009—February 12, 2009: Full Summary of Provisions" (2009), http://
finance.senate.gov/press/Bpress/2009press/prb021209.pdf (accessed January 23, 2011).

13. Urban-Brookings Tax Policy Center, "Tax Stimulus Report Card, Conference Bill, as of February 13, 2009" (2009), http://www.urban.org/publications/411839.html (accessed January 26, 2010).

14. CBS News/NY Times Poll, "The Tea Party Movement," February 5–10, 2010, http://www
.cbsnews.com/htdocs/pdf/poll_Tea_Party_021110.pdf (accessed March 1, 2010).

15. Schatz, "Obama's Budget Proposal Alters the Typical Tax and Spend Equation," 480–81;
U.S. Congressional Budget Office, "An Analysis of the President's Budgetary Proposals for
FY 2010" (2009), http://www.cbo.gov/ftpdocs/102xx/doc10296/TablesforWeb.pdf (accessed
June 15, 2010).

16. Joint Committee on Taxation, "Estimates of Federal Tax Expenditures for Fiscal Years

2005–2009" (2005), http://www.jct.gov/publications.html?func=select&id=5 (accessed January 29, 2011).

17. Philip Rucker, "Obama Defends Push to Cut Tax Deductions for Charitable Gifts," *Washington Post*, March 26, 2009, A02.

18. CBS/AP, "Top Dems Question Tax Deduction Proposal," *CBS News/Politics*, http://www.cbsnews.com/stories/2009/03/05/politics/100days/economy/main4844012.shtml (accessed January 29, 2010).

19. Schatz, "Obama's Budget Proposal Alters the Typical Tax and Spend Equation," 480–81.

20. Charles McMillan, "Letter to Honorable Barack Obama, from National Association of Realtors," February 26, 2009, http://www.realtor.org/government_affairs/mortgage _interest_deduction/mid_obama_budget_proposal (accessed January 29, 2010).

21. National Association of Realtors, "In This Issue: March 2009 Update," *Eye on the Hill*, 2009, http://www.realtor.org/fedistrk.nsf/4fca10aeb5e60f4f86257414007015d5/582f268be308a762 852575770063330e?OpenDocument (accessed January 29, 2010).

22. Mortgage Bankers Association, press release, "MBA Raises Concern over Limit on Mortgage Interest Deduction in Federal Budget," February 27, 2009, http://www.mbaa.org/ NewsandMedia/PressCenter/67934.htm (accessed January 28, 2010); Amy Hoak, "This Week's Real Estate Stories," *Marketwatch: Real Estate Weekly*, February 27, 2009.

23. Center for Responsive Politics, "Real Estate: Money to Congress," OpenSecrets.org, http:// www.opensecrets.org/industries/summary.php?ind=F10&recipdetail=A&sortorder =U&cycle=2008 (accessed April 12, 2011).

24. Center for Responsive Politics, "Non-Profits, Foundations, and Philanthropists," OpenSecrets.org, http://www.opensecrets.org/industries/indus.php?ind=W02 (accessed April 11, 2011).

25. For example, Holly Hall, "Charitable-Giving Plan Divides Nonprofit Groups and Worries Donors," *Chronicle of Philanthropy*, March 2, 2009, http://philanthropy.com/article/ Charitable-Giving-Plan-Divides/63030/ (accessed January 29, 2010).

26. Stephanie Strom, "Limiting Deductions on Charity Draws Ire," *New York Times*, February 27, 2009, http://www.nytimes.com/2009/02/27/us/27charity.html (accessed January 29, 2010).

27. Suzanne Perry, "Meaning of Senate Language on Charitable Deductions in Eye of Beholder," *Chronicle of Philanthropy*, April 3, 2009, http://philanthropy.com/blogs/ government-and-politics/meaning-of-senate-language-on-charitable-deductions-in -eye-of-beholder/10961 (accessed January 30, 2011).

28. U.S. Senate Finance Committee, "Description of Policy Options: Financing Comprehensive Health Care Reform: Proposed Health System Savings and Revenue Options," May 20, 2009, http://finance.senate.gov/sitepages/leg/LEG%202009/051809%20Health%20Care %20Description%20of%20Policy%20Options.pdf (accessed January 29, 2010).

29. Barack Obama, "Transcript: President Obama's News Conference," *New York Times*, March 23, 2009, http://www.nytimes.com/2009/03/24/us/politics/24text-obama .html?pagewanted=all (accessed January 29, 2010).

30. Association for Healthcare Philanthropy, "Coalition Statement to Chairman Max Baucus," June 30, 2009, http://www.ahp.org/Resource/advocacy/us/giftstaxesIRS/ taxdeductibilitycharitablegiving/Documents/AHPCoalitionLetterTaxDedCharGiving063009 .pdf (accessed January 29, 2010).

31. Suzanne Perry, "Senators Propose Charitable Deduction Limits in Health Bill," *Chronicle*

of Philanthropy, September 23, 2009, http://philanthropy.com/article/Senators-Propose/63157/ (accessed January 30, 2011).

32. John Thune, "Press Release: Thune Urges Colleagues to Protect Charitable Giving Tax Deduction," November 5, 2009, http://thune.senate.gov/public/index.cfm?FuseAction=PressReleases.Detail&PressRelease_id=4abf3fb7-0854-4f3d-988f-893223356a6c&Month=11&Year=2009 (accessed January 29, 2010).

33. For source and coding information, see chapter 4, note 45.

34. Obama, "Transcript: President Obama's News Conference," March 23, 2009.

35. National Association of Realtors, "In This Issue: 2009 NAR Public Policy Accomplishments," in *Eye on the Hill*, 2009, http://www.realtor.org/fedistrk.nsf/4fca10aeb5e60f4f86257414007015d5/5ac57ca353ec4a3885257685007b4540?OpenDocument (accessed January 28, 2010).

36. Robert Wood Johnson Foundation, "Talking about Quality, Part I: Health Care Today" (2009), http://www.rwjf.org/pr/product.jsp?id=45110 (accessed March 1, 2010).

37. Garfinkel, Rainwater, and Smeeding, "A Re-examination of Welfare States and Inequality in Rich Nations."

38. Families USA Foundation, "Americans at Risk: One in Three Uninsured," Washington, DC (2009), http://www.familiesusa.org/assets/pdfs/americans-at-risk.pdf (accessed January 28, 2010).

39. Gould, "Employer-Sponsored Health Insurance Erosion Accelerates in the Recession"; Katherine Swartz, "Uninsured in America: New Realities, New Risks," in *Health at Risk: America's Ailing Health System—and How to Heal It*, ed. Jacob S. Hacker (New York: Columbia/SSRC, 2008), 32–65.

40. Cathy Schoen, Jennifer L Nicholson, and Sheila D. Rustgi, "Paying the Price: How Health Insurance Premiums Are Eating Up Middle-Class Incomes," *The Commonwealth Fund*, data brief, August 2009, http://www.commonwealthfund.org/~/media/Files/Publications/Data%20Brief/2009/Aug/1313_Schoen_paying_the_price_db_v3_resorted_tables.pdf (accessed January 28, 2011).

41. Jacob S. Hacker, "The New Push for American Health Security," in *Health at Risk*, ed. Hacker, 106–37; Blumenthal and Morone, *The Heart of Power*.

42. Center for Responsive Politics, "Lobbying, Ranked Sectors," OpenSecrets.org, http://www.opensecrets.org/lobby/top.php?indexType=c (accessed January 30, 2011).

43. Jill Quadagno, *One Nation, Uninsured: Why the U.S. Has No National Health Insurance* (New York: Oxford University Press, 2005).

44. Hacker, *Divided Welfare State*, 188, 207.

45. Quadagno, *One Nation, Uninsured*, 22–24.

46. Ibid., 50; Jennifer Klein, *For All These Rights: Business, Labor, and the Shaping of America's Public-Private Welfare State* (Princeton, NJ: Princeton University Press, 2003), 177–85.

47. Hacker, *Divided Welfare State*, 203, 239–42.

48. Gottschalk, *Shadow Welfare State*; Quadagno, *One Nation, Uninsured*, chap. 2.

49. Hacker, *Divided Welfare State*, 214.

50. Gottschalk, *Shadow Welfare State*; Theda Skocpol, *Boomerang: Health Care Reform and the Turn against Government* (New York: Norton, 1997), 78–80.

51. Quadagno, *One Nation, Uninsured*, 189–94, quote on 189; Skocpol, *Boomerang*, 133–42; Jacobs and Shapiro, *Politicians Don't Pander*, 131–46.

52. Lawrence R. Jacobs and Theda Skocpol, *Health Care Reform and American Politics: What Everyone Needs to Know* (New York: Oxford University Press, 2010), 69–70.

53. Ibid., 70–71.

54. Robert Pear, "In Divide over Health Care Overhaul, 2 Major Unions Withdraw from a Coalition," *New York Times*, March 6, 2009, http://www.nytimes.com/2009/03/07/us/politics/07health.html (accessed January 29, 2011); David Glendinning, "AMA Backs House Health System Reform Bill that Includes Medicare Pay Overhaul," July 27, 2009, http://www.ama-assn.org/amednews/2009/07/27/gvll0727.htm (accessed January 29, 2011); J. James Rohack, "AMA Reaction to President Obama's Address on Health System Reform," September 9, 2009, http://www.ama-assn.org/ama/pub/health-system-reform/news/september-2009/obama-health-reform-address.shtml (accessed January 29, 2011); Kim Gieger and Tom Hamburger, "Healthcare Reform Wins over Doctors Lobby," *Los Angeles Times*, September 15, 2009, http://articles.latimes.com/2009/sep/15/nation/na-lobbying-ama15 (accessed January 29, 2011).

55. Karen Tumulty and Michael Scherer, "How Drug-Industry Lobbyists Won on Health Care," *Time*, October 22, 2009, http://www.time.com/time/politics/article/0,8599,1931595,00.html (accessed January 29, 2010); Tom Hamburger, "Obama Gives Powerful Drug Lobby a Seat at the Health Care Table," *Los Angeles Times*, August 4, 2009, http://articles.latimes.com/2009/aug/04/nation/na-healthcare-pharma4 (accessed January 29, 2011); Sheryl Attkisson, "White House and Big Pharma: What's the Deal," *CBS News*, August 10, 2009, http://www.cbsnews.com/stories/2009/08/10/eveningnews/main5231143.shtml (accessed January 29, 2011); Jeffrey Young, "AARP Endorses House Healthcare Reform Bill," *The Hill*, November 5, 2009, http://thehill.com/homenews/house/66533-aarp-endorses-house-healthcare-bill (accessed January 30, 2011); Jeffrey Young, "Reid Vows Help for Medicare Drug Costs," *The Hill's Blog Briefing Room*, December 14, 2009, http://thehill.com/blogs/blog-briefing-room/news/72221-reid-vows-help-for-medicare-drug-costs (accessed January 30, 2011).

56. America's Health Insurance Plans, "AHIP Statement on Cost Containment Framework," May 11, 2009, http://www.ahip.org/content/pressrelease.aspx?docid=26969 (accessed January 29, 2011).

57. Jacobs and Skocpol, *Health Care Reform and American Politics*, 72; Peter H. Stone, "Health Insurers Funded Chamber Attack Ads," *National Journal*, January 12, 2010, http://undertheinfluence.nationaljournal.com/2010/01/health-insurers-funded-chamber.php (accessed January 29, 2011).

58. Jacobs and Skocpol, *Health Care Reform and American Politics*, 73; emphasis added.

59. Rick Klein, "Labor on Line in Health Care Debate," ABC News, September 7, 2009, http://abcnews.go.com/Politics/labor-line-health-care-debate/story?id=8492718 (accessed January 29, 2011); Alec MacGillis, "Obama Rallies Labor in Fight for Health-Care Reform," *Washington Post,* September 16, 2008; Jacobs and Skocpol, *Health Care Reform and American Politics*, 71.

60. Steven Greenhouse, "Dennis Rivera Leads Labor Charge for Health Reform," *New York Times*, August 26, 2009, http://www.nytimes.com/2009/08/27/business/27union.html (accessed January 29, 2011).

61. Stone, "Health Insurers Funded Chamber Attack Ads."

62. Jacobs and Skocpol, *Health Care Reform and American Politics*, 133–34, 140–41.

63. Ibid., 122.

64. For source and coding information, see chapter 4, note 45.

65. Barack Obama, "Remarks by the President in Town Hall on Health Care," August 14, 2009,

http://www.whitehouse.gov/the_press_office/Remarks-by-the-President-in-town-hall-on -health-care Belgrade Montana (accessed February 26, 2010).

66. Barack Obama, "Remarks by the President in an Online Town Hall on Health Care," July 1, 2009, http://www.whitehouse.gov/the_press_office/Remarks-of-the-President-in-an -Online-Town-Hall-on-Health-Care-Reform (accessed February 26, 2010).

67. Robert Blendon, "Keep an Eye on Public Opinion," *Kaiser Health News*, http://www .kaiserhealthnews.org/Columns/2009/November/110909Blendon.aspx (accessed January 29, 2011); Robert J. Blendon and John M. Benson, "The American Public and the Next Phase of the Health Care Reform Debate," *New England Journal of Medicine*, November 4, 2009, http://healthpolicyandreform.nejm.org/?p=2253 (accessed January 28, 2011).

68. Benjamin I. Page and Robert Y. Shapiro, *The Rational Public: Fifty Years of Trends in Americans' Policy Preferences* (Chicago: University of Chicago Press, 1992), 129–30; Page and Jacobs, *Class War?*, 63–67.

69. Blendon and Benson, "American Public."

70. Henry J. Kaiser Family Foundation, *Kaiser Health Tracking Poll: March 2010*, Chartpack, p. 2, http://www.kff.org/kaiserpolls/upload/8058-C.pdf (accessed December 2, 2010).

71. Mark Schlesinger, "Economic Insecurity and Support for Health and Social Policies: An Evidence Base for Self-Evident Economic Truths" (paper presented at the Annual Meeting of the American Political Science Association, Washington, DC, September 2–5, 2010).

72. Parija Kavilanz, "Health Reform's Immediate Impact: Your Benefits," CNNMoney.com, http:// money.cnn.com/2010/03/26/news/economy/health_care_changes_to_employer_benefits/ index.htm (accessed December 2, 2010).

Chapter Six

1. Kevin Sack, "For Many Families, Health Care Relief Begins Today," and "Chronically Ill, and Covered," *New York Times*, September 23, 2010, A16.

2. Jacob S. Hacker and Carl deTorres, "OpChart: The Health of Reform," *New York Times*, September 23, 2010, http://www.nytimes.com/interactive/2010/09/23/opinion/ 20100923_opart.html (accessed December 3, 2010).

3. "61% Favor Repeal of Health Care Law," *Rasmussen Reports*.

4. PBS Newshour, "Obama on Midterm Shellacking: 'It Feels Bad,'" transcript, November 3, 2010, http://www.pbs.org/newshour/bb/politics/july-dec10/obama_11-03.html (accessed December 3, 2010).

5. McCarty, Poole, and Rosenthal, *Polarized America*, chap. 2.

6. Betty Houchin Winfield, *FDR and the News Media* (New York: Columbia University Press), 121. Winfield calculates listening rates ranging from 59 percent of Americans on December 29, 1940, to 79 percent on December 9, 1941.

7. Nielsen Wire, "43 Million Watch President Obama's State of the Union Address," January 26, 2011, http://blog.nielsen.com/nielsenwire/media_entertainment/43-million-watch -president-obamas-state-of-the-union-address/# (accessed January 30, 2011).

8. Markus Prior, *Post-Broadcast Democracy: How Media Choice Increases Inequality in Political Involvement and Polarizes Elections* (New York: Cambridge University Press, 2007).

9. Arthur Conan Doyle, "Silver Blaze," in *The Treasury of Sherlock Holmes* (Radford, VA: Wilder Publications, 2007), 214.

10. Individuals can elect to receive the EITC incrementally throughout the year in the form of slightly higher paychecks, but as of 2005 only .02 percent of that total amount refunded had been paid in that way: most take the lump-sum refunds. Steve Holt, "The Earned Income Tax Credit at Age 30: What We Know," *Brookings Institution*, February 2006, 6.

11. Gerald Prante, "Most Americans Don't Itemize on Their Tax Returns," *Fiscal Facts*, July 29, 2007, Tax Foundation, http://www.taxfoundation.org/research/show/22499.html (accessed December 5, 2010).

12. Eric M. Patashnik, *Reforms at Risk: What Happens after Major Policy Changes Are Enacted* (Princeton, NJ: Princeton University Press, 2008), 19.

13. Fay Lomax Cook, Lawrence R. Jacobs, and Dukhong Kim, "Trusting What You Know: Information, Knowledge, and Confidence in Social Security," *Journal of Politics* 72 (April 2010): 14.

14. Sarah Torian, "State and Local Support for Earned Income Tax Credits (EITC) Campaigns," prepared for the Annie E. Casey Foundation, March 2006, http://www.nlc.org/ASSETS/64CE7DAF646445BD9313FCC276644728/IYEF_EITC_State_Local_Support.pdf (accessed January 30, 2011).

15. I am grateful to Dan Carpenter for pointing this out to me.

16. Christopher Howard, *The Welfare State Nobody Knows: Debunking Myths about U.S. Social Policy* (Princeton, NJ: Princeton University Press, 2007), chap. 1.

17. For example, Report of the Century Foundation Working Group on Tax Expenditures, *Bad Breaks All Around* (New York: Century Foundation Press, 2002).

18. Tami Luhby, "Mortgage Tax Break in the Cross-Hairs," CNNMoney.com, December 2, 2010, http://money.cnn.com/2010/12/02/news/economy/mortgage_interest_deduction/index.htm (accessed January 30, 2010).

19. "Highlights of the Tax Package Signed into Law," *CQ Weekly*, December 27, 2010, 2941.

INDEX